S

£2·00

D0236367

POPE, DICKENS, AND OTHERS

POPE, DICKENS

and Others

*

ESSAYS AND ADDRESSES

*

JOHN BUTT

EDINBURGH
at the University Press
1969

© Mrs E. M. Butt 1969
EDINBURGH UNIVERSITY PRESS
22 George Square, Edinburgh 8
North America
Aldine Publishing Company
320 West Adams Street, Chicago
Australia and New Zealand
Hodder & Stoughton Ltd
Africa, Oxford University Press
India, P. C. Manaktala & Sons
Far East, M. Graham Brash & Son
85224 031 7
Library of Congress
Catalog Card Number 68-58906

Printed in Great Britain
by W and J Mackay and Co Ltd, Chatham

* Foreword *

This volume is another cairn commemorating that greatly lamented scholar, teacher, and friend John Butt. It is the better that the stones are of his own hewing, worth preservation for their own sake as well as for their illustration of his qualities and characteristics.

Three are concerned with his main subjects, Pope and Dickens. They are sighting shots or breakings of ground, preliminaries to the work which most occupied him. It seemed a natural attraction, to Pope for his good sense and his scrupulous art, to Dickens for his emotional warmth and his enjoyment of rhetoric; to both for their unfailing sense of the life around them. He found in Izaak Walton another example of that same humanity—the pleasure in observation and the pleasure of congenial company. He was like that himself. It is not incidental or irrelevant; and—with all respect to the late school of critical puritanism and that other which regards lucidity and good writing as signs of intellectual debility—it is a quality that has produced much of the best criticism in all ages. I never heard him speak of Shelley, but I fancy he was not one of those who are fascinated by Shelley's withdrawals into abstract distance. It was not that he was narrow in his interests; as is shown by the essay in which he discusses the relationship, of which translation is a clear indication, of such diverse poets as Pope, Milton, and Herrick

to the humane artist Horace; and by his sound understanding of the balance James Thomson kept between
physical science and human life.

The note on Mrs Wolley's treatises on cookery and
household management is incidental, a by-product, but
it is not irrelevant: it contains another piece of evidence on the society which produced the literature he
worked over. Many journalists have exploited similar
subjects, usually to arouse horror and derision. John
Butt had more sense and better manners: he understood
the values of the good housewife and could not mock
this respectable lady, but presents us blandly with a portrait like Hogarth's studies of his housemaids and the
shrimp-seller. His wide and various reading for the
volume of the Oxford History of English Literature, on
which he laboured so cheerfully and gallantly to complete in pain and deadly sickness, might have produced
more such excursions in bypaths; but it was not to be.
I regret particularly that he did not live to do more in
the field opened in the lecture on music and poetry –
that is, on song: it has fascinated me these forty years
and more. Something has been done, but there is much
more to do. John Butt had the gifts for it: a wide and
penetrating knowledge of poetry, and a cultivated
knowledge of music; and, with these, a rich, sympathetic voice well trained both in the declamation of verse
and in singing. Thus he knew not only the theories and
the documents, but the other essential thing – the sensa-
tions that performance produces in the breathing and
vocal muscles, and the controls to be observed. This
essay should be recorded on tapes or discs. The scraps
of music are not interpolations, or interruptions by
another person, but quotations like any other quotations, that exemplify without breaking the unified
progress for either lecturer or hearer.

I have left the first essay to the end, for fear of
leaving the reader with the notion that the work was
all pleasure and self-indulgence. Behind it all lay the

exact and painstaking scholar, as anxious to ensure a true grasp of meanings as he is to ensure the correct textual transmission of his author's text. He quotes also his experience with a student. It is one that any careful teacher must have met, for it takes long reading to habituate oneself to the exact values of shifting terms–*idea* in Spenser, *affections* in Wordsworth–and see that they are not obscured by the apprentice worker.

Here then we have this memorial to a scholar, critic, historian, teacher, and citizen of the world. I am indeed happy to be allowed to affix this little tablet.

W. L. Renwick, FBA
Professor Emeritus of Rhetoric and English Literature
University of Edinburgh
July 1968

It is clear that John Butt would not himself have published some of the essays in this volume in their present form; and readers should always bear in mind the date at which each essay was written. Even without the extensive revision which only he could have undertaken, however, the material seemed far too attractive to leave unpublished. A very few editorial notes have been added to bring the text up to date, and references have been given whenever this seemed helpful. Slight changes in phrasing have been made in one or two places where the original seemed more appropriate to a lecture than to the printed page. The text of the quotations has in general been made to conform to that of standard editions.

The Editors of the *Durham University Journal* and of *The Dickensian* have kindly consented to the republication of material which originally appeared in those periodicals ('A Plea for More English Dictionaries' and 'Science and Man in Eighteenth-Century Poetry' in the *Durham University Journal*, and 'Dickens's Christmas Books', in part, in *The Dickensian*). The University of California Press have also kindly given permission to reprint the essay on Izaak Walton, which was the first of the Ewing Lectures for 1962, published as *Biography in the hands of Walton, Johnson, and Boswell* (Los Angeles 1966). The other essays are printed from MS: 'English

Music and English Verse' was originally delivered to a meeting of the Southampton Branch of the English Association, 2 June 1939; 'The Domestic Manuals of Hannah Wolley' was prepared for a meeting (in 1931) of the Buckingham Mothers' Union; 'The Imitation of Horace', in the form printed here, was read to a group in Downing College, Cambridge, in December 1939; 'Pope and the Opposition to Walpole's Government' was read to a similar group in King's College, Newcastle upon Tyne in 1946; 'Dickens's *Christmas Books*' was given to a meeting at the Literary and Philosophical Society of Newcastle upon Tyne in 1951; and 'The Serial Publication of Dickens's Novels' was read to a summer school at Madingley Hall, Cambridge, in 1958.

Mrs E. M. Butt, Mr Robin Gilmour, Miss W. M. Maynard, Professor Geoffrey Tillotson and Professor Kathleen Tillotson have been generous in their help in preparing these essays for the press. Mr Alan Bell read the proofs and prepared the greater part of the index. To him, and to the editorial department of the Edinburgh University Press, I am deeply indebted.

Geoffrey Carnall

Contents

A Plea for More English Dictionaries

The last time I heard the question of Compulsory Philology discussed, a modernist was uttering the customary complaint that the philologist is so much concerned with his roots that he has no time to give to the flowers. This remark provoked a reply from one of our most learned medievalists. 'Your assumption', he said, 'seems to be that we medievalists should study the modern forms of the language. But why should we? We are not medievalists because we are interested in philology; we have become philologists because we recognize that we must thoroughly understand the language of the writers we are studying. It is up to you whose interests lie in more recent times to be your own philologists. You seem to know what you need as much as we do. Then why not set about it?'

This seemed to me a sensible contribution to the dispute; but when we begin to follow the advice and look round upon what needs doing, the prospect is so vast that we may well feel discouraged. In English studies we have, it is true, the help of the *Oxford English Dictionary*; but as soon as we narrow our linguistic enquiries to one small tract of time we soon recognize what limited assistance that great work can give. Some years ago I asked an Honours student to examine the scope of Dryden's vocabulary as manifested in certain of his plays. Even in the short time at his

disposal he discovered half-a-dozen words of which
there is no record at all in the Oxford Dictionary and
a dozen more of which the Dictionary's first recorded
instance was fifty to a hundred years after Dryden's
death; and that was in addition to the evidence of
boldness in adjectival formations and in figurative
extensions of meaning which I suspected he would
discover. He was naturally inclined to censure the
Dictionary. If he, after a few weeks' part-time work,
could detect so many oversights, how many more
were there likely to be? I was able to persuade him that
though the Dictionary ought to have included those
words and noted those earlier instances, it was not
surprising that omissions should be found, considering
the field the editors undertook to cover; and that what
he had been doing showed rather the lack of some other
important tools. It showed how much we need both a
dictionary of seventeenth-century English and a
Dryden concordance–that is to say, a dictionary to
show us the potential scope of Dryden's vocabulary,
and a concordance to show us the actual scope. A
dictionary of seventeenth-century English might well
do more. It might tell us something about relative
frequency in the use of certain words; it might tell us
in what measure Milton restored words long out of use
to the poetic vocabulary, and to what extent he imposed
his diction on Dryden and subsequent poets.

Unbeknown to my student or to me, Mr E. A.
Horsman was also at work on Dryden's vocabulary at
much the same time. But whereas my student had been
chiefly attracted by Dryden's use of contemporary
slang and cant words, Mr Horsman's attention had
been drawn to Dryden's French borrowings. Here, one
might have supposed, was a field of study which had
already been sufficiently well covered. Dr Johnson, in
the Preface to his *Dictionary*, called attention to the
rage for gallicisms, wanton innovations which had so
long been infecting the language that he thought we

should soon be reduced to babble a dialect of France. And of course we have long recognized the popularity of French manners and French fashions after the Restoration, and have observed in the words which Etherege puts into the mouth of his fop in *The Man of Mode* and in the words which Dryden gives to Melantha in *Marriage-à-la-Mode* the temporary effect which this fashion was having upon the language. But Mr Horsman found not merely several French words used by Dryden some years before their earliest occurrence recorded by the Oxford Dictionary – words such as *brunette*, *dupe*, *embarrass*, *incontestable*, and such a phrase as *carte blanche* – but he was able to show[1] that Dryden's gallicisms enabled him to express his meaning more perfectly, and were not used merely to gain a laugh at the expense of contemporary affectations. The adjustment Mr Horsman has made in the history of the language in the late seventeenth century is small but significant, and it illustrates the need both for similar examinations of the vocabularies of other contemporary writers and of a more precise pronouncement upon the deficiency in the language which these gallicisms supplied.

A somewhat different case could be made out for a dictionary of Tudor and Elizabethan English. In several respects it is a stronger case, for meanings are more obscure and dialectical survivals more frequent. Such a book would show the limited scope of our language as a vehicle for learned works at the beginning of the sixteenth century and the richness of its capacity at the end. In part this is known already. Most Honours students of English could write a paragraph or two about 'inkhorn terms', and many could write much more – of Caxton and his choice of dialect, of the purist views of Cheke, Hoby, and Wilson, of the *Shepheardes Calendar* and of E.K. This has been familiar for many

[1] 'Dryden's French Borrowings' *Review of English Studies*, N.S. i (1950) 346–51.

years, and latterly our knowledge of the principles which guided sixteenth-century translators and scientists in their choice of words has been enlarged, notably by Miss Sweeting's examination of sixteenth-century Bible translations in her *Studies in Early Tudor Criticism*, and by Professor Francis R. Johnson, who in an article in *Studies in Philology*[1] has shown how the word of Latin derivation was preferred to the word of Saxon derivation in sixteenth-century scientific terminology. Just as in our Bible translations *centurion* was preferred to Sir John Cheke's suggestion of *hundreder*, and *apostles* to his *frosent*, so in geometry *equilateral* was preferred to *threelike*, and *tangent* to *touchline*.

In most of these studies mention is made of Sir Thomas Elyot, a humanist of the same generation as Sir Thomas More, a man greatly interested in classical theories of education and eager to place them within the reach of English readers, much interested too in the classical moralists and anxious to share his reading in them with those of his countrymen who knew neither Latin nor Greek. His work is largely translation, or paraphrase, or exposition of classical texts; and that is true of his medical treatise *The Castel of Helth*, in which he attempts to summarize the advice of Galen, Hippocrates and others, at the same time commenting on it in the light of his experience in physicking himself.

No account of 'inkhorn terms' is complete without reference to Elyot's neologisms. But owing to the inaccessibility of his writings, it is not so generally recognized that his work as a translator reveals the inadequacy of early Tudor English as a vehicle for philosophic and scientific thought. There is, it is true, a remarkably fine edition of his principal work *The Gouernour* (1531), published (alas) too early for the editor to make use of the *Oxford English Dictionary*, and American presses have reprinted three of his other

[1] April 1944.

books, *The Castel of Helth, Of the Knowledge which maketh a Wise Man*, and *The Defence of Good Women*; but of his remaining writings no edition has been published since the sixteenth century.[1]

Elyot was an exceptionally self-conscious writer; and perhaps it is owing to his legal and philosophical training that he was also exceptionally cautious in weighing his words and defining his terms. His work is therefore admirably suited to reveal the scope of the English vocabulary at the beginning of the sixteenth century. He himself was not a little proud of the additions he had made to the language, and he tells us in the preface to *Of the Knowledge which maketh a Wise Man* that no less a reader than Henry VIII had approved what he had done:

His highnesse benignely receyuynge my boke,
whiche I named the Gouernour, in the redynge
therof sone perceyued that I intended to augment
our Englyshe tongue, wherby men shulde as well
expresse more abundantly the thynge that they
conceyued in theyr hartis . . . hauynge wordes
apte for the pourpose: as also interprete out of
greke, latyn or any other tonge into Englysshe,
as sufficiently as out of any one of the saide
tongues into an other. His grace also perceyued
that through out the boke there was no terme new
made by me of a latine or frenche worde, but
it is there declared so playnly by one mene
or other to a diligent reder, that no sentence
is therby made derke or harde to be vnder-
stande.

His methods of explaining 'derke or harde termes' were various. There is the open admission of the barrenness of the English language at a certain point, followed by

---

[1] But see *Four Political Treatises*, ed. L. Gottesman (Gainesville, Florida 1967), which reprints the text of the first editions of *The Doctrinal of Princes, Pasquil the Playne, The Banket of Sapience*, and *The Image of Governance*.

the term as used in another language, and its representation in English. Thus he writes in *The Castel of Helth*:

> I wyl somewhat wrytte of two discrasyes of the body, whiche doo happen by the excesse or lacke of thynges callyd not naturall, whereof I have spoken before. The one is callyd cruditie, ye other lassitude, whyche althoughe they be wordes made of latyne, hauynge none apte englyshe worde therefore, yet by the defynytions and more ample declaration of them, they shall be vnderstande suffycyentely, and from henceforth vsed for englysshe.[1]

Or to take an example, from his dialogue *Pasquil*: Pasquil asks Harpocrates to teach him 'what ye calle imminent, for it is a worde taken out of latyne, and not commenly vsed'. To which Harpocrates replies,[2]

> Mary the thynge that is imminent, is whan it appereth to be in the instante to be done or to happen: and after some mens exposition, as it thretned to come.

a definition which satisfies Pasquil, who remarks 'It is well expouned and clerkly'.

Sometimes Elyot contents himself with coupling an unusual word with its nearest common equivalent. Thus he will write 'then shall he, in redyng tragoedies, execrate and abhorre the intollerable life of tyrantes'[3] or 'some lawes by addyng to sondry opinions, be . . . inuolued or wrapped in doubtis,'[4] and on turning up *execrate* and *involve* in the Oxford Dictionary our suspicion of their novelty in 1531 is confirmed by finding that the earliest instances of those words are dated 1561 and 1643 respectively.

This device of coupling nearly equivalent terms, one of Saxon the other of Romance origin had been

---

[1] ed. 1541, f. 74b.
[2] *Pasquil* (1533) f. 19.
[3] *The Gouernour*, ed. H. H. S. Croft (1880) i, 71.
[4] *Of the Knowledge*, ed. E. J. Howard (Oxford, Ohio 1946) 136.

used already by Caxton, and long before by Chaucer and by even earlier writers. Thus in a thirteenth-century text we read 'cherité þet is luve', 'ignoraunce þet is unwisdom and unwitnesse', and in Chaucer 'my herte and my corage', 'huntynge and venerye'.[1] The device is peculiarly well suited for use at a time when a language is rapidly growing, and when a writer may reasonably doubt whether a new term has been acclimatized or whether it has yet displaced a rival.

Occasionally Elyot will leave the classical word unaltered where it seems to him neither to admit of translation nor to submit to an anglicized form. Thus he writes in *The Gouernour*:

in an oratour is required to be a heape of all maner of lernyng: whiche of some is called the worlde of science, of other the circle of doctrine, whiche is in one worde of greke *Encyclopedia*,[2]

and subsequent practice has confirmed Elyot's doubt of the possibility of anglicizing the term. He has been confirmed too in retaining the Greek word in the following passage:

take away ordre from all thynges what shulde than remayne? Certes nothynge finally, except some man wolde imagine eftsones *Chaos*: whiche of some is expounde a confuse mixture.[3]

But he need not have been so cautious with another Greek word, which has been much bandied about since he first transliterated it:

An other publique weale was amonge the Atheniensis, where equalitie was of astate amonge the people, and only by theyre holle consent theyr citie and dominions were gouerned . . . This maner of gouernaunce was called in greke *Democratia*, . . . in englisshe the rule of the comminaltie.[4]

[1] F. Mossé *Esquisse d'une histoire de la langue anglaise* (1947) 94.
[2] i, 118.
[3] ibid., 3.
[4] ibid., 9–10.

We may detect him too in the act of using an uncommon, if not a freshly minted, word when he
introduces a term with a note of apology, as for example,
'the consideration is wonderfull excellent, and to be
(as I mought saye) supersticiously obserued'[1] or 'all
whiche wordes, if they be intierly and (as I mought
saye) exactely understanden.'[2] The first use recorded
by *O.E.D.* both of *superstitiously* and *exactly* is a few
years later than the date of Elyot's book.

When I first began to read Elyot I was content to
notice the carefully defined terms, the couplings of
seemingly uncommon and familiar words, the conscious
transliterations and translations, and the intruded
apologies. But I had not gone far before I recognized
that these devices did not necessarily denote the
introduction of new words. Elyot's philosophical
training made him careful to define even such old
words as *Abundance* and *Necessity*; and his coupling of
nearly equivalent terms often seems merely to bespeak
the precision of a man bred to the law. Elyot's signals,
then, do not always draw attention to a new word; but
I also found that new words, or what the Oxford
Dictionary would have us believe were new words,
were introduced without signals. Here was a problem.
In such a sentence as this there is no sign to show the
presence of an uncommon word–'they speke none
englisshe but that which is cleane, polite, perfectly and
articulately pronounced'[3]–yet there is no earlier
recorded instance of the word *articulate*. Similarly I
have found Elyot using the word *emulation* on two
occasions,[4] on neither of which does he show any
consciousness that the word is dated twenty years later.
Since it is impossible for a man to use a new word without some consciousness of what he is doing, we can

1 *The Gouernour*, ii, 341–2.
2 ibid., 226.
3 *The Gouernour*, i, 35.
4 ibid., 69; *Bibliotheca*, 1545, Aiii[r].

only conclude that the evidence collected by the Oxford Dictionary is insufficient as to the number of texts consulted and in the examination of the texts themselves. More could not have been expected of the Dictionary considering the extent of the field it covers: what I am pointing out is that we need a series of supplementary dictionaries covering smaller portions of the field in greater detail and with more lavish quotation.

Greater detail might throw some light on another peculiarity. Though Elyot uses the word *emulation* quite familiarly, the verb *emulate* is not found until the 1590s. That is quite credible. We should not necessarily expect the need for the verb to be felt immediately after the noun was coined. But can we believe that 120 years could elapse between the coining of the word *aggravation* and the formation of its verb? The evidence of the Oxford Dictionary seems to point to such an interval; but we can reduce it by fifty years on finding the verb in Elyot's *Pasquil*,[1] and that immediately renews our doubts about the interval of time which seems to separate the first uses of *emulation* and *emulate*. Or again, we find that *tolerance* and *tolerable* have been in the language since the early fifteenth century, but the verb *tolerate* is first recorded in the writings of Elyot and More one hundred years later. We need the guidance of the more specialized dictionary with its ampler volume of illustrations before we dare say that the need for the verb was first felt in the sixteenth century.

¶ I now pass to the type of words which Elyot used or thought he was using for the first time, and shall begin with what can be gleaned from *The Castel of Helth*. It is to be expected that an early vernacular medical treatise would be the first to introduce a large number of medical terms. It is to be expected, not only because it is one of the first in the field, but because the renewed

[1] ed. cit., f. 26r.

study of classical medical texts at that time revealed deficiences in the vernacular. Elyot is to be seen filling those gaps in *The Castel of Helth* and conscientiously defining for his unlearned readers such terms as *adustion*[1] and *crudity*[2] which we no longer require, as well as such, to us, every day words as *temperature* and *dispense*[3] (in the sense of making up a medicine according to a prescribed formula). The presence of so many words needing definition must have made the book most laborious reading for an unlearned sixteenth-century Englishman, but Elyot appears so little conscious of this that he even prefers an unfamiliar term to an exactly equivalent familiar. Thus the word *gargle* was in use in Elyot's day and admirably serves its purpose both by virtue of its meaning and of its sound, yet Elyot nevertheless chooses to adopt the learned formation *gargarize*[4] from Galen. Again, *digestion* is cognate with the word used by the classical physician Celsus for the process by which food is assimilated into the system; and a suitable word it is, too, with its implications of separating, dissolving, and distributing. The word was known to Elyot and his readers, but he prefers a more unfamiliar word *decoction*. We can watch him in the process of accustoming his reader to it – 'continuall studie', he writes, 'hyndereth naturall decoction and digestion'.[5] Here the explanation of Elyot's choice seems to be that he, like other physiologists of his time, regarded the liver as the fire which heats the pot of the stomach, and the process of digestion is therefore apprehended to be a process of cooking. A word, therefore, which carries a metaphor of cooking is to be preferred to one that does not.[6]

---

[1] ed. cit., f. 6a.   [2] ibid., f. 74b.   [3] ibid., Aiii[r].
[4] ibid., f. 90a.   [5] *The Gouernour*, i, 169.
[6] Further reflection makes me doubtful of this explanation. Andrew Boorde in his *Dyetary* (1542) uses the term *decoct* on only one occasion, so far as I have found: 'he can not naturally nor truely decocte, defye, ne dygest, the superabundance of meate'

We also find Elyot succumbing in *The Castel of Helth* to the temptation which seems to beset doctors, the preference for a learned term where the layman would suppose that a common term would serve equally well. It is to Elyot that we owe *masticate*[1] for *chew* and *eructation*[2] for *belch*, and he also offered *distillations*[3] in substitution for *rheums*. Medical colleagues to whom I have put the question have not found much use for *masticate*;[4] but one can sympathize with the desire to substitute *eructation*, a word sterile of associations, for the more vulgar term.

It is generally supposed that Elyot's non-medical neologisms are of the same kind, that is to say, terms of learned origin preferred to terms in common parlance. Certainly many of his coinings have fallen into disuse; several of them were never adopted by his contemporaries; but while that is evidence of failure, it is no evidence that the need for some equivalent term was not felt. The word *adminiculation* is a case in point. The Latin *adminiculum* is the stake or prop upon which the vine was trained, and was used by Cicero with its verb in a figurative sense. Elyot defines the word in his Latin dictionary as 'aid, supportation', and uses it in anglicized form in the following context:

> . . . suche men, hauyng substance in goodes by certeyne and stable possessions . . . may . . . cause [their children] to be so instructed and furnisshed towarde the administration of a publike

---

(ed. 1870), p. 250. This seems to imply that Boorde is distinguishing three physiological processes, 'cooking,' dissolving, and digesting. The term he normally uses in his *Dyetary* is *digest*, e.g., 'old pecockes be harde of dygestyon'. This, taken with instances in Elyot, suggests that whereas *digestion* was used to cover the whole process of assimilation, *decoction* was confined to what goes on in the stomach.

[1] *The Banket of Sapience* (1534) A3ʳ.

[2] *Castel*, f. 41b.

[3] ibid., ff. 77b, 78a.

[4] To one of them the word conveyed the process of salivation as well as that of chewing.

> weale, that a poure mannes sonne, onely by his
> naturall witte, without other adminiculation or
> aide, neuer or seldome may atteyne to the sem-
> blable.[1]

Aid in that context is not the equivalent of *adminicula-tion*. Elyot has in mind the training a boy needs for the service of the state, and he sees that the boy requires like the vine some stake or prop, such as a wealthy father can supply, to help him in his earliest years. Today we should probably use the word *support*; but the Oxford Dictionary's evidence suggests that *support* was not used in that sense till the end of the seventeenth century, and that the obsolete forms *supportation* and *supportance* were not in general use till the end of the sixteenth. There was, it seems, a gap in the language which Elyot recognized and attempted, not too successfully, to fill. Do we detect a difference here between the Tudor humanist and the less learned Elizabethan? Who can doubt that Shakespeare, or even Nashe, feeling the need of such a word would not have appealed to his native sense of metaphor before apply-ing to the resources of a learned language? Elyot's use of the word *maturity* provides a further illustration:

> [Of celeritie and slownesse] springeth an excellent
> vertue where unto we lacke a name in englisshe.
> Wherfore I am constrained to usurpe a latine worde,
> callyng it *Maturitie*: whiche worde, though it be
> strange and darke, yet by declaring the vertue in a
> fewe mo wordes, the name ones brought in custome,
> shall be as facile to understande as other wordes
> late commen out of Italy and Fraunce, and made
> denizins amonge us.
>
> Maturitie is a meane betwene two extremities,
> wherein nothing lacketh or excedeth, and is in
> such astate that it may neither encrease nor
> minisshe without losinge the denomination of
> Maturitie. The grekes in a prouerbe do expresse it

[1] *The Gouernour*, i, 27.

> proprely in two wordes, which I can none other
> wyse interprete in englisshe, but speede the slowly.
> Also of this worde Maturitie, sprange a noble
> and preciouse sentence . . . Consulte before thou
> enterprise any thing, and after thou hast taken
> counsaile, it is expedient to do it maturely.
> *Maturum* in latine maye be enterpreted ripe or
> redy, as frute whan it is ripe, it is at the very
> poynte to be gathered and eaten. . . . Therfore
> that worde maturitie is translated to the actis of
> man, that whan they be done with suche modera-
> tion, that nothing in the doinge may be sene
> superfluous or indigent, we maye saye, that they
> be maturely done: reseruyng the wordes ripe and
> and redy to frute and other thinges seperate from
> affaires, as we haue nowe in usage. And this do I
> nowe remembre for the necessary augmentation of
> our langage.[1]

Why attempt, we may ask, to acclimatize the word
maturitas when we already had *promptness* and *promptitude*
to hand? But were they? The first recorded instance of
prompt is a mere hundred years before Elyot was writing.
Promptly is first found forty years before his time,
promptitude eighty years, and *promptness* five. They had
arrived, in fact, but they could scarcely be regarded as
established; and in these circumstances a term already
well established in a classical language had an obvious
appeal. We know, of course, that *prompt* eventually displaced *mature*; but *mature*, *maturity*, and *maturely* are
used in Elyot's sense by Shakespeare and Milton, and
indeed to the end of the eighteenth century. Elyot was,
in short, making a sensible contribution to the language.

Elyot showed the same power of recognizing gaps
in the vocabulary of ethical and social concepts and
had a much greater measure of success in filling them.
To him we owe–or rather, in default of more detailed

[1] ibid., 242–5.

lexicographical information we appear to owe—the following terms: *activity, audacity, beneficence, clemency, education, equability, frugality, implacability, imprudence, liberty of speech, loyalty, magistrate, mediocrity, sincerity,* and *society*.[1]

It is remarkable to be able to credit one man with so many important additions to the language which statesmen and moral philosophers need in their daily business; and it is a striking reflection both upon the poverty of the language in the fifteenth century and of the suddenness of the demand upon the language in the early sixteenth that most of these words should appear for the first time in one book and all of them in the fifteen years between 1530 and 1545. The care which Elyot took in making the more important of these additions is remarkable, and may be illustrated by his introduction of the word *modesty*, in a sense which has since become obsolete:

> . . . the vertue called Modestie, whiche by Tulli is defined to be the knowlege of oportunitie of thinges to be done or spoken, in appoyntyng and settyng them in tyme or place to them conuenient and propre. Wherfore it semeth to be moche like to that whiche men communely call discretion. Al be it *discretio* in latine signifieth Separation, wherein it is more like to Election; but as it is communely used, it is nat only like to Modestie, but it is the selfe Modestie. For he that forbereth to speake, all though he can do it bothe wisely and eloquently, by cause neither in the time nor in the herers he findethe oportunitie, so that no frute may succede of his speche, he therfore is vulgarely called a discrete persone. Semblably they name him discrete, that punissheth an offendour lasse than his merites

---

[1] *The Gouernour*, i, 194; ii, 263; ii, 90; *The Doctrinal of Princes*, 1534, f. 19b; *The Gouernour*, i, 24; ii, 329; ii, 336; ii, 59; *Of The Knowledge*, p. 26; *Doctrinal*. f. 11a; *The Gouernour*, ii, 225; i, 25; i, 289; *The Image of Governance*, 1541, f. 36a; *The Gouernour*, ii, 201.

do require, hauyng regarde to the waikenes of his
persone, or to the aptnesse of his amendement. So
do they in the vertue called Liberalitie, where in
gyuynge, is had consideration as well of the
condition and necessite of the persone that
receiuethe, as of the benefite that comethe of the
gyfte receyued. In euery of these thinges and their
semblable is Modestie; whiche worde nat beinge
knowen in the englisshe tonge, ne of al them which
under stode latin . . . they improprely named
this vertue discretion. And nowe some men do as
moche abuse the worde modestie, as the other dyd
discretion. For if a man haue a sadde countenance
at al times, and yet not beinge meued with wrathe,
but pacient, and of moche gentilnesse, they whiche
wold be sene to be lerned, wil say that the man is of
a great modestie; where they shulde rather saye
that he were of a great mansuetude; whiche terme,
beinge semblably before this time unknowen in our
tonge, may be by the sufferaunce of wise men
nowe receiued by custome, wherby the terme shall
be made familiare. That lyke as the Romanes
translated the wisedome of Grecia in to their citie,
we may, if we liste, bringe the lernynges and
wisedomes of them both in to this realme of
Englande, by the translation of their warkes; sens
lyke enterprise hath ben taken by frenche men,
Italions, and Germanes, to our no litle reproche for
our negligence and slouth.[1]

It is the self-consciousness of the language-making
which renders the passage so interesting, and the
anxiety Elyot shows that he should be precisely understood. But was he always understood by the reader who
had no Latin? This is a question which can only be
settled after similar studies of Elyot's contemporaries.
I am aware as I read him of the need of testing the
language-making of Wyatt and Sir Thomas More.

[1] *The Gouernour*, i, 267–9. *Mansuetude* is at least as old as Chaucer.

How did they face the problem of rendering the classical moralists into Tudor English? Did they too find the vernacular deficient, or deficient in the same places? What were their methods of filling the gaps? These questions could and should be extended beyond the sixteenth century; for what the poet and the moralist have to say in every age is conditioned in part at least by the scope of the language in that age. Our standard dictionary, in attempting so much, presents us with a false record of the language as it has been written and spoken at any one time, and in limiting itself, necessarily, to an average of one instance in fifty years it smudges the distinction between the familiar and the uncommon. The work of supplying this demand is enormous; but we should reach it if we appended a critical glossary to every text we edit, a glossary which should take into account not merely the shift in meaning of words in common use but the effect of that shift upon closely related words. By this means I hope we should gradually reach a keener sense of the potentiality of the language at various periods in our history.

1951

2

English Music and English Verse

The kinship of poetry and music has often been announced. Milton, for example, regarded the two arts as 'sphear-born harmonious Sisters', and Barnfield, writing some years earlier, found it impossible that there could be any disagreement between such close relatives. Poetry and music have taken divergent paths since those days, but the basis of their agreement remains the same, for the materials in which they work are still rhythm, stress, and pitch. By rhythm, I mean the systematic grouping of notes or words; by stress, I mean the degree of emphasis given to word or note either by weight, or by its position in a rhythmical phrase, or by the length of the pause which precedes or succeeds it; by pitch, I mean the height at which a word or a note is sounded. It may be said that so far as poetry is concerned, none of these three things is of primary importance, that it would still be possible for the poet to effect some degree of communication without a systematic grouping of words, and that the opportunity of writing and printing poems has reduced the importance of stress and pitch. There is some truth in the objection, and the fact that such an objection can be made shows how far poetry and music have diverged, for music has never and could never be freed from these three fundamentals. Nevertheless, I believe it would be true to say that in the greater part of even the freest verse the poet has subjected his words to some system of grouping; and I believe most poets have wished their verse to be read aloud, a condition which immediately involves the use of stress and pitch.

So little is one accustomed to considering the importance of rhythm, stress, and pitch in poetry, that perhaps it may be apposite to recall a famous passage in *Macbeth*, the precise meaning of which is uncertain because Shakespeare failed to give sufficient directions for speaking it—in other words, for rhythm, stress, and pitch. The scene is the seventh of Act I, where Lady Macbeth is endeavouring to strengthen Macbeth's purpose. Macbeth is hesitant: 'If we should fail?' he asks. To which Lady Macbeth replies—and it is necessary to read her words as unrhythmically, unemphatically, and monotonously as one can—

> We fail:
>
> But screw your courage to the sticking place,
> And wee'll not fail.

I grant that even so some communication is made. The drift of the speech is clear. But what is the precise meaning of the two words 'We fail'? Is Lady Macbeth scornful, or is she incredulous, or does she accept the suggestion only to dismiss it in her next sentence? If she is incredulous, she will pitch the word WE pretty high, she will drop about a musical sixth for FAIL, and rise perhaps a tone before leaving it. If she is scornful, she will pitch WE rather low, and drop even lower, a semitone or a minor third, to FAIL. But if she is momentarily accepting the suggestion, she will make an upward leap of at least a semitone, perhaps even a fourth. The three possibilities could be represented somewhat roughly in musical script:

The size of the intervals might change a little from performance to performance; but the broad distinctions between the three possibilities would remain the same. It is only necessary to add that if these words had appeared in the libretto of an opera, the music to which they were set—by reason of the inescapable concern which music has with rhythm and pitch—would immediately resolve any doubt of the correct emotional interpretation.

This passage from *Macbeth* is by no means a solitary example of the difference which rhythm, stress, and pitch can make in a poet's meaning. I will venture to quote one more. Pope's *Eloisa to Abelard* is a highly rhetorical poem, in which a number of contrasting pictures are elaborated so as to exasperate the conflict in Eloisa's mind. Eloisa as a nun should have surrendered all thought of her profane passions on taking the veil. She cannot do so, and in her agony she envies the blameless Vestal's lot, whose golden dreams are prompted by whispering angels, and who melts in visions of eternal day. She proceeds to contrast her own experience:

> Far other dreams my erring soul employ,
> Far other raptures of unholy joy.

I should explain that we have reached a point more than halfway through the poem, and that it is no longer sympathetically possible to read such lines in an unimpassioned way. The reader *must* declaim them; he *must* begin to distribute his rhetorical stresses; but where? Did Eloisa wish to emphasise the emotional distance which separated her from the blameless vestal? Or did she wish to emphasise how *different* her dreams were? Or did she wish to scourge her erring soul? In other words, should the reader stress F A R, O T H E R, or E R R I N G? Should he read the passage like this?

> F A R other dreams my erring soul employ,
> F A R other raptures of unholy joy.

or like this?

> Far OTHER dreams MY erring soul employ,
> Far OTHER raptures of unholy joy.

or like this?

> Far other dreams my ERRING soul employ,
> Far other raptures of UNHOLY joy.

The drift of the passage remains the same in these three possible emotional interpretations. Had the words been set to music, the emotional interpretation would not have been open to conjecture. Either by stress or by pitch or by a combination of the two, the composer would have settled the question once for all. We should be deprived of the pleasure of ambiguity, but in return we should acquire a new deepening of the emotion selected. From such examples one might generalize with some hesitation and say that the poet is incapable of communicating the finest shades of meaning without the assistance of the musician, who (incidentally) is incapable of communicating meaning at all, as we generally understand it, without the help of the poet.

But the basis of agreement between music and poetry is not confined to rhythm, stress, and pitch. The medium of the two arts is the same. Whereas the painter may be said to work in the medium of space, the poet and the musician work in the medium of time. The painter presents at once all that is needed for receiving what he has to communicate. One may require time to study it, to relate the parts to the whole; but he keeps nothing back. Now the poet and the musician, by the very nature of their arts, have always something to keep back. They rely upon the memory for their contrasts and their climaxes, and since they must arrange their contrasts in time rather than in space, and since they must prepare for their climaxes over a period of time, it would seem reasonable to suppose that there is some similarity in the forms they use.

But there is a difference between the value of time for the poet, and its value for the musician, a difference which can be put very briefly. The musician requires more time than the poet to establish communication with his audience. That is a faulty generalization: one has only to remember the first eight notes of Beethoven's Fifth Symphony to see that a musician can establish communication as rapidly and forcibly as any poet. I should have said that a musician who follows a poet, as a song composer follows a song writer, cannot express his partner's verbal ideas with any precision; he can only induce the same mood which the words are expressing, and it takes him longer than the poet to do this. But I am aware that even in this modified form the generalization is not completely sound. There is at least one brilliant exception in the *Messiah*. When Handel proceeded to set the words 'I know that my redeemer liveth', he devised a musical theme which commences with the upward leap of a fourth, an interval which often seems to carry with it a sense of elated conviction. The first listeners to *Messiah* would not *know* that Handel was about to announce his conviction that his 'redeemer liveth', but they would be sure that he was about to express elated conviction about something. I hope for the sake of my generalization that this will be found to be a brilliant exception. As a rule one would not expect a musician to establish the mood of dejection caused by unrequited love, for instance, as quickly as the poet can say 'Gentle Love! Draw forth thy wounding dart'.

Those words are from a song set by John Dowland in 1597. Let us see what problems the poet and musician have given each other. The first verse of the song is as follows:

Come again! sweet love doth now invite
Thy graces, that refrain

> To do me due delight,
> To see, to hear, to touch, to kiss, to die
> With thee again in sweetest sympathy.

The first three lines do not offer any remarkable
opportunity to the composer; he must simply follow
the poet, which he does by preserving the rhythm of
such a phrase as 'Come again', and stressing the
importance of 'love, who invites' by pitching the
word 'love' rather high. But the fourth line is a gift
which Dowland makes the most of. He sets it to a
series of rising fourths, which give the impression of
palpitating with excitement because they start half a
beat later than the heavy rhythmical beats (see
example opposite).

So far the association has been one of give and take,
which appears (all the same) to be one of perfect agreement. Troubles begin to arise in the later verses, for
since the convention was to keep the same verse form
and the same setting throughout the song, poet and
composer must agree to give and take in exactly the
same places. And the burden is now all upon the poor
poet, for the composer, having written a setting for one
verse, makes no further modifications. For the first
rhythmical phrase in the second verse it is easy to
repeat 'Come again!', and the poet does so. For the
second phrase he must contrive to arrange things, so
that his important stress shall fall on the second note,
since that was the important note in the similar
position of the first verse; and he manages this too:
'that I may cease to mourn'. And he carries this
rhythmical grouping successfully through in every
verse:

> All the day / the sun that lends me shine . . .
> All the night / my sleeps are full of dreams . . .
> Out alas! / my faith is ever true . . .
> Gentle Love, / draw forth thy wounding dart . . .

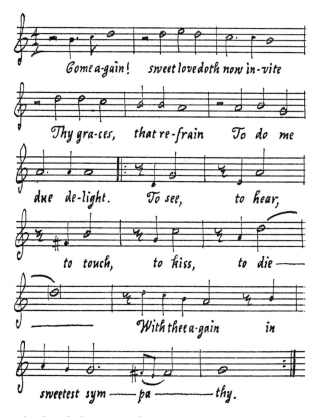

Come a-gain! sweet love doth now in-vite

Thy gra-ces, that re-frain To do me

due de-light. To see, to hear,

to touch, to kiss, to die —

— With thee a-gain in

sweetest sym — pa — thy.

The fourth line proved more troublesome. That was the line which the composer had set to a series of rising fourths, suggesting by this musical conceit the palpitating expectancy of 'To see, to hear, to touch, to kiss'. But the poet can scarcely expect to invent a parallel conceit for each of the five succeeding verses. In the second verse he devises a progression which fits the rhythm, but it is a lugubrious progression—'I sit, I sigh, I weep, I faint, I die'—and is inappropriate to the elation of the music. But after this attempt in the second verse, the poet gives it up entirely, and in the last four verses we find:

Her smiles my springs that makes my joys to
    grow . . .
To see the fruits and joys that some do find . . .
Her eyes of fire, her heart of flint is made . . .
By sighs and tears more hot than are thy shafts . . .

None of which is really suitable for the musical phrase.

This song provides us with a characteristic example of the difficulties which faced the poet and composer in Elizabethan times through the convention of retaining an unchanging air throughout a poem of several verses. The burden would seem to fall upon the poets, many of whom resolved the difficulties with greater success than Dowland's anonymous partner–I assume incidentally that the work was considered as a partnership, and that in those days when England was full of musicians no poet can have entertained the possibility of his lyrics not being set to music. If this is considered too great an assumption, it must at least be admitted that when Shakespeare wrote lyrics for his plays he wrote them with the intention of their being sung, and it is clear that he foresaw this trouble which I have been attempting to expound. He usually makes the rhythmical phrases of one verse correspond with those of the others. Some obvious examples of this correspondence are

Blow, blow, thou winter wind,
Thou art not so unkind
    As man's ingratitude;

which is almost perfectly matched in rhythm, stress, and pitch in the second verse by

Freeze, freeze, thou bitter sky,
That dost not bite so nigh
    As benefits forgot.

Probably the singer would need to manipulate the rhythm in the third line, but otherwise the correspondence is excellent. And so it is in

Come away, come away, death

which is matched in the second verse by

Not a flow'r, not a flow'r, sweet:

'On my black coffin let there be strown' is equivalent rhythmically to 'And in sad cypress let me be laid'.

Fly away, fly away, breath;
I am slain by a fair cruel maid

is very well matched by

Not a friend, not a friend greet
My poor corpse, where my bones shall be thrown.

At this point the equivalence is abandoned, and I cannot guess what the composer would have done with the last four lines of each verse. What he did do is unknown, since no contemporary setting has survived.

There must remain an element of doubt about such reconstructions. For example, it has been suggested that Shakespeare, like Burns, wrote his songs to folk tunes, which might account for the verse forms he used, though I must add that I have never seen any convincing proof of this. It might also be argued that the poem 'Come away, sweet Love doth now invite' was not necessarily written in collaboration with Dowland, and that, therefore, instead of finding fault with the poet, one might equally well blame Dowland for not devising an air which would have suited every verse. We are on safer ground in examining some of the work of Thomas Campion, who is known to have set his own verses to music.

Such study as I have made of Campion's music leads me to think that he paid special attention to this business of equivalence. An example from his *Third*

fix one smile on thee,
Time make way for Love

where were de — spair? The loss is but
through ribs of steel? The Gre - cian en —

ea — sy which smiles can re —
- chan-ted all parts but the

- pair. A stran - ger would
heel. At last a shaft

please thee if she were as fair.
daun-ted which his heart did feel.

Booke of Ayres, 1612, will show this without any
elaborate exposition on my part. The stanza is made
up of five lines, of which the first two and the last two
pair off, and the third asks a question. This disposition
is followed in the second stanza; furthermore, the
caesuras and rhetorical stresses occur in each stanza at
identical places. The music emphasizes the divisions of
the stanzas, underlines the rhetorical stresses, and also
serves to deepen the emotional content of the Ayre (see
pp 26, 27). This was written in 1612, yet in 1646 Milton
was commending Henry Lawes for being the first song-
writer who

> taught our English Musick how to span
> Words with just note and accent, not to scan
> With *Midas* ears, commiting short and long.

In other words, Milton seems to have thought that
Lawes was the first musician to aim at equivalence. The
Elizabethan composers sometimes failed to achieve
equivalence. Even Thomas Morley sometimes failed;
for though he wrote in his *Plaine and Easie Introduction
to Practicall Musicke*, 1597, that musicians must 'have a
care so to applie the notes to the wordes, that we cause
no sillable which is by nature short be expressed by
manie notes or one long note, nor no long sillable be
expressed with a shorte note'. I find him occasionally
transgressing his rule, in his setting, for example, of
such a phrase as 'Sweet nymph, come to thy lover'
(see below). But this is an occasional lapse; and no one

can doubt from Morley's words, or from the practice
of Campion and others, what Elizabethan intentions
were in regard to scanning words with just note and

accent. I do not know what Milton meant; or rather, I am surprised that a poet who habitually wrote with such care and shows on other occasions so much understanding of music could have allowed himself to make such a statement.

But to return to Campion: I suggested that it would seem reasonable to suppose that some similarity could be found between the forms which the poet and the musician use, since they both work in the medium of time, and arrange their contrasts and prepare for their climaxes in that medium. But it appears to be true that musical form and verse form can only resemble each other when each is at its loosest. Campion's stanza did not approximate to any recognized stanzaic form. It consisted of three iambic six-stress lines, followed by two dactylic four-stress lines. The formlessness of this stanza was easy to represent in music for the very reason that it is formless – except for the rhymes, there is no specific verse design to mimic – and Campion can represent this formless stanza by freely moving melodic phrases, each corresponding to the length of a line in the verse, which equally truly bear no resemblance to any known musical form. But as soon as the poet chooses a more definite form he makes it impossible for the musician to represent that form. For example, what can a musician do to represent rhymes? The answer is that he does not think that it is worthwhile representing them. Elizabethan composers do frequently devise conceits to represent assonance in the poem before them, but I remember no examples of their applying this principle to rhymes. Consequently, no verse, such as the sonnet, which depends largely on rhyme for the recognition of its form, can easily be represented in music. The most that a musician will do is to point the end of a line with a cadence, as Campion does in his song 'The peaceful western wind' (see overleaf); but such a practice is by no means regularly observed. The musician can also represent a couplet, as Campion does

The peace-ful west-ern wind The winter storms hath tamed; And Na-ture in each kind The kind heat hath in — flamed.

in 'Break now, my heart, and die', by marking off the constituent lines with cadences, by repeating the setting of the first line for the second line, and by separating the couplet from the rest of the air by means of a change in rhythm. But this also is an exceptional practice, and only serves to show more clearly that the more formal the stanza is, the less able is the musician to represent it.

And the musician has his formal designs, too, which the poet would be unable or unwilling to copy. What use, for example, could a poet have for simple binary or simple ternary form, of which the essence is repetition? The fugue, on the other hand, would appear to be too elaborate for a parallel verse form. De Quincey, it is true, once wrote a fugue in words, at the end of *The English Mail Coach*, but this is an exceptional *tour de force*, which could not be set to music. I think the only musical form which offers any exact correspondence with a poetic form is the Rondo (A B A C A), which corresponds very nearly to the ballads and their refrains written by such poets as Rossetti and Morris.

The musician is thus generally confronted with two choices. Either he can do as Campion did in 'Break

now, my heart, and die', that is, he can follow the form
of the verse, setting each line to a melodic phrase more
or less independent of the rest of the air; or he can
adopt a musical form and thereby sacrifice some degree
of equivalence to the verse. The logical development of
Campion's method is the recitative, in which melody,
fixed rhythms, and recognized musical form are largely
disregarded in favour of a style completely subservient
to the rhythms of the speaking voice. There are several
styles in recitative writing. At one extreme, the
recitativo secco, as it is called, becomes a most useful
device for making mere announcements in opera or
oratorio. Examples of this kind are 'Behold, a virgin
shall conceive' and 'There were shepherds abiding in
the field' from *Messiah*. An announcement is needed and
the business of making it is done with as little fuss as
possible. More elaborate is much of the evangelist's
work in Bach's *St Matthew Passion*, where many of the
announcements are of a highly emotional nature, and
Bach accordingly colours his recitative with florid
decorations which momentarily lose touch with the
verbal rhythms. The best example is Peter's weeping
on hearing the cock crow, which is both an announcement and a description at the same time. Or, as an
English example, I might quote Handel's 'I rage, I
melt, I burn', where the *description* of Polyphemus's
emotion is at least as important as its *announcement* (see
overleaf).

Such work is halfway between *recitativo secco* and a
formal air. It is an example of what is called *recitativo
stromentato*. But this type of recitative can be even
more melodic and formal in its rhythms, as for example
'For Behold! Darkness shall cover the Earth' from
Messiah. I am pretty sure that an Elizabethan, such as
Campion, would have considered such work as an air,
for it follows each verbal phrase in melodic fashion; and
I suppose the only reason why Handel called it a
recitative was that it obeyed none of the laws of musical

form by which he thought an air should be constructed. In fact, Handel found no difficulty when confronted with the two choices which I put before you a moment ago. If he wished to announce something either plainly or emotionally, he used either *recitativo secco* or *recitativo stromentato*; if he wished to set meditative words, he adopted a musical form for the purpose, and usually he adopted a version of simple ternary form. How he managed to avoid sacrificing equivalence altogether I will try to show, after examining a cruder attempt to solve the same difficulty made by Dowland.

In 'Come away, Sweet Love doth now invite', we have seen Dowland following his poet's stanza phrase by phrase and line by line. In other airs, he not only tries to do this but tries to devise a satisfactory musical form at the same time. As an example of such an attempt, I will examine his 'Awake, sweet love, thou art returned'. The stanza is made up of fourteen lines, two exactly similar tercets and two exactly similar quatrains, and this no doubt suggested to Dowland that a suitable musical form for such a stanza would be simple binary form (AABB) (see pp 34, 35). The difficulty comes in suiting the rhythmical and emotional quality of the musical phrases to the rhythmical and emotional quality of the verbal phrases. Complete success might well be impossible. My opinion is that

Dowland has succeeded beautifully in setting the first tercet and the first quatrain of the first verse–that, in fact, his tunes perfectly fit the first words to which they are set; but when these tunes are repeated (in the first verse, and twice in the second verse) they are only approximately equivalent.

I do not think it is possible to make a completely successful blend of stanzaic form, musical form, and verse rhythms, by such straightforward means. I am not surprised at Dowland's failure; I am surprised at the large measure of his success. But compromises are possible, and are perhaps more pleasing. My first example of a compromise is Purcell's famous song 'I attempt from Love's sickness to fly', the verse of which consists of three couplets written in a rather coarse four-stress dactylic measure:

> I attempt from Love's sickness to fly in vain,
> For I am myself my own fever and pain.
> No more now, no more now, fond heart with pride swell;
> Thou canst not raise forces enough to rebel.
> For Love has more power and less mercy than Fate
> To make us seek ruin and love those we hate.

The principal changes which Purcell makes are to convert these couplets into a rondo and to remove the coarseness of the verse rhythm. He converts the couplets into a rondo by repeating the first couplet after the second, and again after the third. Just how he has removed the coarseness of the rhythm is difficult to detect. The use of repetitions and decorative ornaments has certainly helped him in what was evidently his purpose–to reduce the pace of the couplets without losing their briskness. In spite of these changes, Purcell has preserved all that is essential in the poem. He has retained the individuality, the separateness, of the couplets–I think he has even emphasized their individuality; he has preserved the rhythm, stress, and

love; She, on-ly, drave me to des—
end. She on-ly, which did make me

—pair *W*hen she un — kind did prove.
fly, *M*y state may now a — mend.

pitch of the clauses; and he has endowed the words with
a depth of emotion which they could not convey without a musical setting. If one part of such a perfect work
of art is better than another, it is the setting of 'Thou
canst not raise forces enough to rebel'.

I regard this song as a highly successful compromise.
A slight modification is made in the verse form, in
order to produce a satisfactory musical form, the rondo;
but the modification is so slight as not to alter the
essential character of the verse.

But Purcell does not always pay so much respect to
his poet's form. When necessary, he is willing to
sacrifice it, if he thinks a bold and dramatic treatment
would be justified. For his song 'Anacreon's Defeat', he
was provided with a lyric of two seven-line verses
written in the manner of Cowley's anacreontics:

This poet sings the Trojan wars;
Another of the Theban jars,
In rattling numbers, verse that dares.
Whilst I, in soft and humble verse,
My own captivities rehearse.

I sing my own defeats, which are
Not the events of common war.

Nor fleets at sea have vanquish'd me,
Nor brigadiers nor cavalry,
Nor ranks and files of infantry.
No, no, Anacreon still defies
All your artillery companies,
Save those encamp'd in killing eyes;
Each dart his mistress shoots he dies.

Purcell seems to have felt that there was no question of compromise here. For the division into two stanzas, Purcell substitutes a division into *three* parts. He neglects the grouping of lines which the rhymes supply. He dispenses with the lines themselves and with the regular iambic stresses. Nothing of the poet's work is left except the order of the words, which might as well have been written as a block of solid prose. Purcell brushes aside the poet's form to concentrate on his own. The form he chooses may be described as a variant of simple ternary form. Instead of repeating his first theme, following it with a contrasting theme, and concluding with a repetition of the first theme, Purcell contrasts, not themes, but styles. He starts with a violent passage of *recitativo stromentato*, which he repeats. Then follows a contrasting passage in a soothing lyrical style, and to conclude he returns to a fresh outburst of *recitativo stromentato*. Such a musical setting might be described as a free dissertation upon the poet's theme rather than an attempt to follow the poet. And no one could doubt that the boldness and richness of Purcell's contrasts fully justifies the liberties he took.

My last example of a compromise between musical and poetic form is Manoah's air 'How willing my paternal love' from Handel's oratorio *Samson*. The form Handel chooses is the simple ternary form—a theme repeated, followed by a contrasting theme, and concluded by a return to the original theme. I remarked that Dowland in making a similar choice had got into trouble over the repetition of his theme, which did not suit the second portion of his verse as well as it had suited the first portion. Handel ingeniously gets over this difficulty by giving the first announcement of his theme to the orchestra. The voice thus enters at the first repetition, which sets the first four lines of the stanza. The concluding couplet of the stanza is set to the second contrasting theme, and the orchestra rounds off the air with a truncated repetition of the first theme, thus completing the simple ternary form.

In theory, this is a most satisfactory way of harmonizing the poet's and the musician's forms, neither of which should greatly suffer. I must admit, however, that in this air Handel does not take the greatest pains to preserve the poetic form. The individuality of the lines is not well marked; in fact, all that is really obvious in Handel's setting is the distinction between the first half of the stanza and the concluding couplet. There are no bad misapprehensions of English rhythms, such as we find in 'For unto us a child is born' and 'He sha-al feed his flock like a she-e-e-pherd' in *Messiah*; but, on the other hand, there are no remarkable felicities to point out, such as his setting of 'Whatever is, is right' in *Jephtha*, and 'Love in her eyes sits playing' in *Acis and Galatea*. I offer it with these reservations as a not very satisfactory example of the compromise between verse form and musical form.

¶ In this paper I seem to have been generalizing and dogmatizing with a rashness peculiar to those who rush in where more learned people fear to tread, and I am aware that it is pointless to be more careful now in drawing conclusions. I will therefore only hope that I have shown that the marriage between music and poetry must always involve concessions, that one art will almost always dominate the other, that they can scarcely ever be equipoised, in spite of equivalences in rhythms, and that this difficult union produces in the work of such a man as Purcell an artistic effect which is more emotionally rich and rhythmically subtle than either the poetry or the music could produce independently.

1939

NOTE. All who heard John Butt lecture on topics such as this will recall the animation with which he sang and played his own musical illustrations. The quotation from Handel's 'I rage, I melt, I burn', for instance, evokes vivid recollection of his rendering of Polyphemus's song. For this reason the lecture has been given here with only a very few verbal changes to adapt it to print.

Izaak Walton as Biographer

When Bacon made his survey of the state of learning
at the beginning of the seventeenth century, he did not
leave biography out of account. The word itself seems
to have been unknown to him and indeed was not in
common use until after the Restoration, a sign that the
thing itself was still uncommon. It is not surprising,
therefore, that he should find a deficiency in this branch
of learning. He deplores the deficiency; and in doing
so, he defines with his customary precision what virtues
a good biography should possess:

> . . . lives, if they be well written [he says], pro-
> pounding to themselves a person to represent, in
> whom actions both greater and smaller, public
> and private, have a commixture, must of necessity
> contain a more true, native, and lively repre-
> sentation [than narratives of action].[1]

The deficiency was soon to be supplied in ample
measure; for the age was surely conducive to biography
that was so much addicted to investigating the past, to
recording its investigations and its memories, and to
interpreting them. We now recognize that one of the
impulses underlying the antiquarian movements of the
day was the need felt in a time of political and ecclesiastical upheaval to inquire into the wisdom of our
ancestors. Such monuments of seventeenth-century

[1] *Of the Advancement of Learning*, II, ii, 5.

learning as Dugdale's *Monasticon* and Wharton's *Anglia Sacra* subserved the purposes of political and ecclesiastical controversy; but surely these men were also impelled by a purer motive, such a motive as sent John Leland out in the previous century to record those manuscript collections that were in danger of dispersal at the dissolution of the monasteries? For though the antiquaries felt a sense of achievement in their labours, there was a sense of disappointment as well; so much had been irretrievably lost. This sense of disappointment was well expressed by Sir Thomas Browne in the preface of *Urn Burial* (1658), when he wrote:

> 'Tis time to observe Occurrences, and let nothing remarkable escape us; The Supinity of elder dayes hath left so much in silence, or time hath so martyred the Records, that the most industrious heads do finde no easie work to erect a new *Britannia*.

Browne had his fellow antiquaries in mind, as he shows, in a note to this passage commending the excellent endeavours of Sir William Dugdale. But his words could also be read as a call to action on a much wider front: *Our* successors, he seems to say, will have less to complain about *us*, if we now set about our tasks, record the stirring events through which we are passing, and commemorate the great men of our age. It is possible to detect two distinct but related impulses here, both of which have their effect upon biographical writing: one is the commemorative impulse; the other is the need to write the history of our times for the benefit of posterity.

Commemorative biography had been sanctioned by Bacon, who observed in *The Advancement of Learning* that 'there are many worthy personages that deserve better than dispersed report or barren elogies'.[1] This was the motive to which Izaak Walton was most ready to confess. Biography, he says in the Epistle to the

[1] op. cit., II, ii, 9.

Reader of the second collected edition of the *Lives*, is 'an honour due to the dead, and a generous debt due to those that shall live, and succeed us';[1] and for the motto to be set on the title page, he chose a suitable text from *Ecclesiastes* (xliv. 7), 'These were Honourable Men in their Generation'. Walton's first two lives were frankly commemorative. The *Life of Donne* was a 'well-meant sacrifice to his memory',[2] a somewhat hastily produced preface to a great volume of sermons, which would otherwise have been published without the decency of a tribute. It had originally been intended that the memorial preface should be written by Donne's friend, Sir Henry Wotton. But Wotton was dilatory, and death overtook him before his task was performed. Walton succeeded to it, because he had already been employed by Wotton, as he tells us, in gathering material for Wotton to use.

Wotton had died on 9 December 1639, the *Sermons* had been entered on the Stationers' Register on 3 January 1640, and Walton records that he finished the first version of his life on 15 February. Clearly there had not been much time for additional investigation. He had to be content with what he had collected–for Wotton seems to have collected nothing–and with what he already knew. It is obvious that he knew practically nothing about dates. The first to be mentioned is 1630, the year before Donne died, and it was here that Walton was to apply himself when the opportunity arose of revising and expanding his first version. There are quite a lot of dates in Walton's final version, published thirty-five years after his first, and many of them are correct; but the need to supply them, the purpose that dates and records might serve in a biography, was something which Walton was to recognize only late in his career. Today no biographer would think of beginning to write without first compiling a chronological table of his subject's life, firmly

[1] *The Compleat Walton*, ed. G. Keynes (1929), 203.   [2] ibid., 219.

pegged with dates as accurate as he can determine. I see no evidence that Walton began his *Life of Donne* in that way, nor his *Life of Wotton* either; but in his last three lives, those of Hooker, Herbert, and Sanderson, he seems to have made an effort to consult such records as parish, college, and diocesan registers, or to have had them searched for him. He sometimes made mistakes, he sometimes overlooked what a more thorough investigation might have revealed, but it is very much to his credit that he so often recognized the significance of these facts, and overcame obstacles that we cannot readily imagine, living as we do in an age of well-supplied public libraries and well-organized registries. It is to his credit also that, when he was already over sixty years old, he could adapt a manner of biography which had served him well in the *Life of Donne* for the infinitely more complex problems facing him in the *Life of Hooker* and the *Life of Sanderson*, problems involving the interpretation of recent history and the significance of an individual's participation in it.

The mere sequence of historical events in these two lives must have forced the need of some chronological table upon his attention, and the difficulty of compiling it must have been aggravated by the sheer mass of material that could be readily assembled from records, books, and the recollections of friends. This problem did not face him when composing the *Life of Donne*. His subject in this biography was a prominent public figure, but one who had taken no part whatever in affairs of church or state. All that seemed to be required was a memorial tribute to the man who had preached the eighty sermons that followed. In his prefatory remarks Walton quotes from Plutarch's *Life of Pompey*.[1] If some study of Plutarch had helped to form his conception of biography, he would never have been convinced of the need of a firmly delineated chronology; this would not have occurred to him; but like Plutarch,

[1] ibid., 217.

he would have seen his task as the presentation of a literary portrait or the delineation of character through narrated action.

There is some independent evidence about the extent of Walton's acquaintance with Donne. In all probability the two men did not meet before 1624, when Donne was appointed to the living of St Dunstan's-in-the-West in Fleet Street, where Walton kept a draper's shop close by, and was one of the parish officers. At the most, therefore, their acquaintance lasted for seven years, since Donne died in 1631. No letters from Donne to Walton survive; but in a letter from Sir Henry Wotton to Walton, Wotton refers to Donne as 'our ever-memorable friend',[1] and Bishop Henry King in a letter written thirty years after Donne's death said that he thought Walton was present with himself and others at Donne's deathbed.[2] Walton indeed claimed Donne's friendship, but modestly described himself as no more than 'the poorest, [and] the meanest of all his friends'; and in an elegy written on Donne's death, he mentions that he was his 'convert'.[3]

Today our interest in Donne is primarily in the author of the *Songs and Sonnets*, and because of what they mean to us we are led to read Donne's other poetry, secular and religious, and his sermons. But it is not difficult to understand that a man who had heard Donne in the pulpit and knew the ascetic of his last years would have been overpowered by that impression; and if he had seen either of those attractive portraits of Jack Donne, the sensual and elegant young courtier, he must have nodded his head sagely over the prophetic epigraph that Donne had had inscribed in Spanish on one of them, 'How much shall I be changed, before I am

[1] *The Life and Letters of Sir Henry Wotton*, ed. L. P. Smith (Oxford 1907) II, 404.
[2] *The Compleat Walton*, 209.
[3] ibid., 218, 273. Cp. 577.

changed!' The epigram that Walton wrote to be en-
graved under the Marshall portrait when it was used
as a frontispiece for the second edition of the *Poems* in
1635 seems an almost inescapable reflection from the
parishioner who remembered the angel in the pulpit
and the ascetic in the deanery:

> This was for youth, Strength, Mirth, and wit that
> 　Time
> Most count their golden Age; but 'twas not thine.
> Thine was thy later yeares, so much refind
> From youths Drosse, Mirth & wit; as thy pure
> 　mind
> Thought (like the Angels) nothing but the Praise
> Of thy Creator, in those last, best Dayes.
> 　　Witness this Booke, (thy Embleme) which begins
> 　　With Love; but endes, with Sighes, & Teares
> 　　　for sinns.[1]

The future biographer can already be discerned in those
lines. Six more years were to elapse before Sir Henry
Wotton's death called him to review his 'forsaken
Collections';[2] but it is evident that he had already
begun to shape the life into what in modern jargon is
called periods, and I think we may justly add that he
had recognized the value of his subject's writings in
interpreting his life. Donne's book is his Emblem; and
since there is a decorum to be observed in these matters
it is right that the sermons should be preceded by a
life of the preacher.

Nor is this epigram a merely instinctive recognition
of how a commemorative biography should be shaped.
In the first collected edition of Donne's *Poems* (1633)
there is even earlier evidence of Walton's biographical
interest in Donne. He wrote for that volume a long
elegy which shows that he had already begun to conduct
some enquiries. He speaks first of the love poetry and
satire of his youth, adding that these were done 'at his

[1] ibid., 578.　　[2] ibid., 217.

twentieth yeare'. Then after mentioning Donne's 'Crowne of Sacred sonnets', his 'Litany', and his 'Hymnes, for piety and wit Equall to those great grave *Prudentius* writ', Walton continues:

> Spake he all *Languages*? Knew he all *Lawes*?
> The grounds and use of *Physicke*; but because
> 'Twas mercenary wav'd it? Went to see
> That blessed place of *Christs nativity*?
> Did he returne and preach him? preach him so
> As none but hee could do?[1]

These lines show that Walton had later something to correct in his knowledge of Donne – Donne seems never to have gone to Palestine, and several years elapsed between his travels and his taking orders – and he had much still to learn; but they also show that Walton knew more about the order of composition of the poems than could be deduced from the chaotic arrangement of the first edition, that he was already curious about the earlier life of his friend, and had taken some pains to inquire what lay outside his own knowledge. Perhaps it was this curiosity that Sir Henry Wotton had sought to harness, when he first engaged Walton to 'inquire of some particulars that concern'd' the life of Donne. Certainly it was the trait in Walton's character that he shared with Boswell and that gave his work, as it was to give Boswell's, its most distinctive quality. Each of them exercised this curiosity about great men long before he became a biographer. Thus Walton recalls in the preface to his *Life of Hooker* that some forty years earlier he had become acquainted with William Cranmer, great-nephew of the archbishop, and his two sisters, who had had part of their education in Hooker's parsonage at Bishopsbourn, near Canterbury;

> . . . and having [says Walton] some years before read part of *Mr Hookers* Works with great liking and satisfaction, my affection to them made me a

[1] ibid., 576–7. Cp. 272–3.

> diligent Inquisitor into many things that con-
> cerned him; as namely, of his Person, his Nature,
> the management of his Time, his Wife, his Family,
> and the Fortune of him and his.[1]

Nor is this an isolated instance, for he tells us that he
had had many discourses concerning Hooker with
Archbishop Ussher, Bishop Morton, and John Hales, all
of whom had died several years before Walton had
even contemplated writing Hooker's life. It was no
doubt from the Cranmers that Walton obtained that
memorable impression of Hooker at Bishopsbourn:

> . . . an obscure, harmless man, a man in poor
> Cloaths, his Loyns usually girt in a course Gown, or
> Canonical Coat; of a mean stature, and stooping,
> and yet more lowly in the thoughts of his Soul; his
> Body worn out, not with Age, but Study, and
> Holy Mortifications; his Face full of Heat-pimples,
> begot by his unactivity and sedentary life;[2]

and almost certainly it was from the Cranmers that he
derived the even more memorable description of
Hooker's injudicious marriage. It now appears that
Walton was misled about Mrs Hooker's shrewish disposition; and perhaps it is some measure of the
difference between him and Boswell that he was less
critical of the anecdotes that he collected. But the
purpose for which each biographer employed anecdote
is the same. It is with the help of anecdote that each
builds up the character of his subject. Thus Hooker's
pupils remembered how easily they could look him out
of confidence, and his mildness and humility was such
'that his poor Parish Clerk and he did never talk but
with both their Hats on, or both off, at the same time';[3]
and the account of Donne's marriage that Walton had
probably obtained from Bishop King, the only episode
in his early life reported with fullness of detail, seems
to have been designed to illustrate both the passionate
nature at whose excesses Donne was very apt to reluct,

[1] ibid., 330.   [2] ibid., 372.   [3] ibid.

and also what Walton calls the 'strange kind of elegant irresistible art'[1] by which Donne won back his angry father-in-law's favour.

It is for anecdote that Walton, like Boswell, shows the greatest enjoyment. He appreciates the *bon mot* as much as Boswell; he relishes adroitness in reply; and like Johnson he recognizes how valuable such anecdote can be in painting a trait of character. Thus Sir Henry Wotton's 'Nobleness of Mind' was shown in his behaviour to the Emperor Ferdinand the Second, whom he had been endeavouring to reconcile to the restoration of James I's daughter, Elizabeth of Bohemia, to the Palatinate. Though Wotton failed in his mission, the Emperor was so pleased with his conduct as to present him with a diamond worth more than a thousand pounds. Wotton received the jewel 'with all outward Circumstances and Terms of Honour', but the following day he presented it to his hostess on taking leave of her. The Emperor, not unnaturally, was affronted; but when told of this, Wotton replied: 'That though he received [the jewel] with thankfulness, yet he found in himself an indisposition to be the better for any gift that came from an Enemy to his Royal Mistress the Queen of *Bohemia*.'[2]

And Walton shares Boswell's delight in marshalling his characters for some trifling episode that nevertheless places his subject in a pleasing or unusual light. The following Oxford anecdote from the *Life of Sanderson* was possibly obtained from no less a person than the Archbishop of Canterbury, a friend of Walton in his later years:

I must look back, and mention one passage more in [Mr Sanderson's] Proctorship, which is; That *Gilbert Sheldon*, the late Lord Archbishop of *Canterbury*, was this year sent to *Trinity College* in that University; and not long after his entrance there, a Letter was sent after him from his Godfather (the

[1] ibid., 224.   [2] ibid., 304.

Father of our Proctor) to let his Son know it, and
commend his Godson to his acquaintance, and to a
more than common care of his behaviour; which
prov'd a pleasing injunction to our Proctor, who
was so gladly obedient to his Fathers desire, that
he some few days after sent his Servitor to intreat
Mr Sheldon to his Chamber next morning. But it
seems *Mr Sheldon* having (like a young man as he
was) run into some such irregularity as made him
conscious he had transgress'd his Statutes, did
therefore apprehend the Proctor's invitation as an
introduction to punishment; the fear of which
made his Bed restless that night; but at their
meeting the next morning, that fear vanish'd
immediately by the Proctor's chearful countenance,
and the freedom of their discourse of Friends.[1]

The relish of the irony inherent in the situation
indicates Walton's kinship with Boswell and his
instinctive appreciation of an important principle of
biography that Johnson was later to enunciate: 'The
business of the biographer is often to pass slightly over
those performances and incidents, which produce vulgar greatness, to lead the thoughts into domestick
privacies, and display the minute details of daily life,
where exterior appendages are cast aside, and men excel
each other only by prudence and by virtue.'[2]

I have already drawn attention to that early elegy
upon Donne, in which Walton begins to interpret his
subject's career in the light of his writings. Though
his store of anecdotes remained his primary source of
material, he also relied to a considerable extent upon
the evidence afforded by what his subjects wrote. He
draws upon their letters, and even their account books;
he quotes from prose prefaces, and he paraphrases
poems. Perhaps he was not the first biographer to
recognize the potential value of such material; but
certainly he is the first biographer to employ it so

[1] ibid., 473–4.   [2] *Rambler*, no. 60.

extensively. Yet it is in this aspect of his work that Walton has given most offence to modern suscept-ibilities. If he had misquoted, we could have forgiven him; if he had simply seen no purpose in superstitiously binding himself to his author's words when a para-phrase would serve, we should have been ready to understand; but what the modern scholar finds it difficult to stomach is the manipulation of the text of letters and prefaces, and the seemingly convenient omission of passages that point in some direction other than that in which the context is tending. Walton has also been convicted of using, in so far as they were convenient, both Herbert's *Temple* and his *Country Parson* as evidence of Herbert's thoughts and behaviour during the last years of his life at Bemerton.

The use of a subject's imaginative work offers a problem to every biographer. Are the opinions expres-sed in drama or in poetry necessarily the opinions of the writer, or do they more properly belong to an assumed character? I am inclined to think that Walton had asked himself this question in relation both to Donne's poems and to Herbert's. Believing that Herbert regarded *The Temple* as 'a picture of the many spiritual Conflicts that have past betwixt God and my Soul, before I could subject mine to the will of *Jesus my Master*',[1] he felt himself justified in selecting at least six or seven poems for direct quotation or for para-phrase to put into Herbert's mouth. Only two or three are related to specific occasions in Herbert's career; and in this respect Walton showed greater caution than Herbert's nineteenth-century editor, who went so far as to rearrange the poems of *The Temple* into a supposed chronological order illustrating the progress of what he imagined to be Herbert's spiritual biography. Walton was also less reckless than Donne's nineteenth-century biographer, Gosse, who assumed that Donne's *Songs and Sonnets* reflected actual occurrences in the

[1] *The Compleat Walton*, 447.

poet's life. It is conceivable that Walton shared this belief, but abstained from making extensive use of these startling lyrics and elegies in a biography commemorating the saintliness of Donne's later days. But some of the poems are morally unimpeachable, and several, especially of the verse epistles, invite biographical interpretation; yet the fact remains that only four, two secular and two sacred, are related to specific occasions. Though he was certainly misinformed about one of the occasions, Walton's manner of procedure was commendably cautious.

The material both anecdotal and literary was used to support an overall view of his subject's character that almost certainly had been formed before he began to work; and such labour as was subsequently required in searching records or in acquainting himself with historical events and interpreting their sequence was not allowed to obscure it. This cannot be convincingly demonstrated; but I have already shown Walton formulating his view of Donne in epigram and elegy; in the following biography the tone seems to have been dictated by the mellowness of Sir Henry Wotton's last years spent as Provost of Eton, the years when Walton got to know him; while in the *Life of Herbert*, the reader is encouraged to see the future model of a parish priest even in the schoolboy at Westminster, where

> the beauties of [Herbert's] pretty behaviour and
> wit, shin'd and became so eminent and lovely in
> this his innocent age, that he seem'd to be marked
> out of piety, and to become the care of Heaven,
> and of a particular good Angel to guard and guide
> him;

and at Cambridge, where

> God still kept his soul in so holy a frame, that he
> may, and ought to be a pattern of vertue to all
> posterity; and especially, to his Brethren of the
> Clergy.[1]

[1] ibid., 407, 412.

Indeed it is difficult to see how Walton at that time could have proceeded otherwise in a century when the character as a literary form had invaded historiography, satire, and the comedy of manners–I have in mind those brief character-sketches in the plays of Ben Jonson and Congreve, where one personage in the drama describes to another the character of a third who is about to enter or to leave the stage for the first time–and when the character achieved an independent existence in the Theophrastan character-sketch. At such a time a biographer would feel every encouragement to see his subject in terms of a character and so to present him.

¶ If we turn for a moment to some other seventeenth-century biographers we shall see how heavily they relied on the set character. Thus in the *Life of Hammond* written by John Fell, Bishop of Oxford, the character is set apart from the narrative and occupies more than a quarter of the whole work. In Evelyn's *Life of Mrs Godolphin*, the character occupies about one-third of the whole, and in Fell's *Life of Fuller* and Bishop Burnet's *Life of Sir Matthew Hale* it is so extensive as to be longer than the narrative itself. The character, in fact, was regarded as an essential appendix to the biography.

> After I have Recounted . . . her *Life* [wrote
> Evelyn of Mrs Godolphin], I should, according to
> the Usual Method, Conclude it with her *Character;*[1]

and Burnet held the same view:

> Having thus given an Account of the most
> remarkable things of his Life [he writes in his *Life
> of Hale*], I am now to present the Reader with
> such a Character of Him, as the laying his several
> Virtues together will amount to.[2]

This practice survived into the eighteenth century. It accounts for Johnson's appending a character to his narrative in the *Lives of the Poets* wherever the material

[1] *The Life of Mrs Godolphin*, ed. H. Sampson (1939) 84.
[2] *The Life and Death of Sir Matthew Hale* (1682) 118.

warranted it. Boswell, too, knew that a character was
expected of him; but he also recognized that it should
have been unnecessary, as his apology shows:

> The character of Samuel Johnson [he writes] has,
> I trust, been so developed in the course of this work,
> that they who have honoured it with a perusal, may
> be considered as well acquainted with him. As
> however, it may be expected that I should collect
> into one view the capital and distinguishing features
> of this extraordinary man, I shall endeavour to
> acquit myself of that part of my biographical
> undertaking, however difficult it may be to do
> that which many of my readers will do better for
> themselves.[1]

'The evidence is already before you,' he seems to say;
'. . . you can deduce the character as well as I.'
Neither Evelyn nor Burnet seems ever to have contemplated dispensing with the character; but it is
interesting to observe that Fell had given some
thought to the question, though he eventually decided
that the character offered him the most effective
method of organizing his material:

> 'Tis easily to be presum'd [he wrote, at the end of
> the first section of his *Life of Hammond*] the Reader
> will not be disoblig'd, if we a while divert from
> this remaining sadder part of the undertaken
> Narrative, and entertain him with a Survey of the
> Personal accomplishments of the Excellent *Doctor*.
> The particulars whereof would not readily have
> faln into the thred of History, or at least had been
> disjoynted there, and under disadvantage; but
> will be made to stand in a much fairer light, when
> represented to the view by way of Character and
> Picture.[2]

[1] *Life of Johnson*, ed. G. B. Hill and L. F. Powell (Oxford
1934) IV, 424–5.
[2] *The Life of the Most Learned Reverend and Pious Dr H.
Hammond* (1661), 83–4. Cp. *The Works of Dr Hammond* (2nd ed.
1684) I, xiii.

This points to the prestige that the character-sketch exerted over the biographer at this time, encouraging him to set out with an image of his subject that could be expressed in terms of the Theophrastan character-writer's short title. Burnet may protest that he is not 'making a Picture of [Hale], from an abstracted *Idea* of great Virtues, and Perfections', but is 'setting him out, as he truly was',[1] yet in fact he sees him as a Theophrastan Upright Judge, just as Evelyn sees Mrs Godolphin as a Young Saint; and Walton sees Herbert as the Good Parish Priest. With this image in view the biographer is encouraged so to select, arrange, and organize his material as to impose this interpretation on his subject.

But was any other procedure possible if unity of tone and emotional colour was to be achieved? Could we expect Walton, or any other biographer, to refrain from reshaping words and actions; and if he had done so, would the result have been impossibly incoherent and meaningless? This question faces us when we consider Boswell; and it is worth glancing at the practice of a contemporary of Walton's, whose procedure was more empirical–I mean John Aubrey. He understood his task to be the collection of evidence for another man's use, and he may therefore be said to hold no responsibility for what was done with the evidence he assembled. He was quite conscious of the disorder of his collections:

> Sir! [he wrote to Anthony Wood, at whose
> instigation much of his work was done] I have,
> according to your desire, putt in writing these
> Minutes of Lives tumultuarily, as they occurr'd
> to my thoughts or as occasionally I had information
> of them. They may easily be reduced into order at
> your leisure.[2]

'Tumultuarily' is the apt adverb he uses on another

---

[1] op. cit., 118.
[2] *Aubrey's Brief Lives*, ed. O. L. Dick (1949) cxiii.

occasion to describe what he has 'many yeares since
collected', adding that 'it may be an Incitement to
some Ingeniose and publick-spirited young Man, to
polish and compleat, what I have delivered rough
hewen'.[1] Yet once at least, in his *Life of Hobbes*, he
set himself to put his collections into order, and produced a memorable portrait to which no Theophrastan
label could possibly be attached. Though Aubrey was
not capable of taking the measure of Hobbes's mind,
what he preserved gives some indication of how that
mind worked. It is surely of some importance to have
this record of the way *Leviathan* was written:

> He sayd that he sometimes would sett his thoughts
> upon researching and contemplating, always with
> this Rule that he very much and deeply considered
> one thing at a time (*scilicet*, a weeke or sometimes a
> fortnight). He walked much and contemplated,
> and he had in the head of his Staffe a pen and inke-
> horne, carried always a Notebook in his pocket,
> and as soon as a notion darted, he presently entred
> it into his Booke, or els he should perhaps have
> lost it. He had drawne the Designe of the Booke
> into Chapters, etc. so he knew whereabout it
> would come in.[2]

Scarcely less valuable is the statement that though
Hobbes had read much,

> his contemplation was much more then his
> reading. He was wont to say that if he had read as
> much as other men, he should have knowne no
> more then other men.[3]

But where Aubrey excels is in his recollection of the
individualities of Hobbes's appearance and behaviour.
We learn that Hobbes shaved close, except for 'a little
tip under his lip'; and the reason follows:

> Not but that nature could have afforded a venerable
> Beard, but being naturally of a cheerfull and
> pleasant humour, he affected not at all austerity

[1] ibid., xxi.   [2] ibid., 151.   [3] ibid., 154.

« 54 »

and gravity to looke severe. He desired not the
reputation of his wisdome to be taken from the
cutt of his beard, but from his reason.

Two other details of appearance are similarly related to
disposition and character:

He had a good eie [we are told], and that of a
hazell colour, which was full of Life and Spirit, even
to the last. When he was earnest in discourse,
there shone (as it were) a bright live-coale within
it. He had two kinds of lookys: when he laugh't,
was witty, and in a merry humour, one could
scarce see his Eies; by and by, when he was serious
and positive, he open'd his eies round (i.e. his
eie-lids).

Even Hobbes's bald head served to show his cheerful
humour:

In his old age he was very bald (which claymed a
veneration) yet within dore, he used to study,
and sit bare-headed, and sayd he never tooke cold
in his head, but that the greatest trouble was to
keepe-off the Flies from pitching on the baldnes.[1]

Aubrey's purpose was to preserve some fragments
against the shipwreck of time. He was afraid that some
detail might be considered superfluous; but on sub-
mitting his draft to friends, they advised him

to let all stand; for though to soome at present it
might appeare too triviall; yet hereafter 'twould
not be scorned but passe for Antiquity.[2]

It was good advice, though it scarcely amounts to a
fully considered theory of biography. Aubrey does not
attempt a character of Hobbes; but I can find no
evidence for his believing that a character-sketch was
superfluous. Yet untidy as it is, the *Life of Hobbes* is
more dynamic than those gracious and statuesque
memorials erected to their friends by Evelyn, Burnet,
and Fell; it tells us almost all we need to know of

[1] ibid.   [2] ibid., xci.

Hobbes at the same time as it shows him going about his business.

I think it is possible to detect in Walton, also, some desire to modify a too precisely formulated approach to character. Thus only one of his lives is concluded with a character-sketch, and that is the *Life of Donne*. When we consider the prominence of the character in contemporary biography, this is surely remarkable. The only prominence that Walton gives to his character of Donne is the italic type in which it is printed, for it occupies no more than one of the eighty pages in the last revised edition.

There is, indeed, something approximating to a character in the four remaining lives, but the handling of the material shows Walton's superior artistry. Whereas Fell brought Fuller 'to his repository, and laid him in his silent Grave' before performing 'some further offices due to his yet speaking Vertues and Graces',[1] it was Walton's habit to conduct his subject to the place of his principal activity, or to the place where Walton was best acquainted with him, and there to describe his behaviour and to illustrate his character by anecdote and recollected conversation.

Some of this material serves to modify, and I believe was intended to modify, the otherwise too Theophrastan consistency of Walton's biography. The outline of Herbert's portrait reveals the good parish priest; the *Life of Donne* is controlled by that vision of the Angel in the Pulpit seen by his humble parishioner; and Hooker and Sanderson are seen as meek but effective defenders of the rights of the Church against the encroachments of Puritanism. Such are the principal impressions we gain from these lives; but they are impressions that do not take into account Walton's ironic enjoyment of the evidences of human imperfection. God may have kept Mr Herbert's soul in a holy

---

[1] *The Life of Dr Thomas Fuller* (1661) 65. Cp. Fuller's *Church History of Britain*, ed. J. S. Brewer (Oxford 1845) I, xxxiii.

frame at Cambridge, but it was not so holy as to
prevent him from neglecting his duties as public
orator: '. . . he enjoyed his gentile humor for cloaths,
and Court-like company, [we are told] and seldom
look'd towards *Cambridge*, unless the King were there,
but then he never fail'd.'[1] The cutting edge is scarcely
as sharp even as that which Chaucer applied to his
Prioress, but it is just perceptible. A biographer with
greater care for consistency might well have been
tempted to conceal the fact that Herbert's 'gentile
humour' for gay clothes and a sword was pursued, in
direct contravention of the rubric, after he had been
admitted to deacon's orders, that Herbert was over-
zealous in reproving the indecencies of behaviour at
divine services, and that he 'put too great a value on
his parts and Parentage'.[2] Not so Walton; and a
biographer with a blunter sense of the value to be
placed on human protestations would not have risked
spoiling the climax of Herbert's holy dying with an
appendix on the subsequent career of Mrs Herbert.
We are told that

> *She continu'd his disconsolate Widow, about six years,*
> *bemoaning her self, and complaining,* That she had lost
> the delight of her eyes; *but more,* that she had lost
> the spiritual guide for her poor soul; *and would often*
> *say,* O that I had like holy *Mary,* the Mother of
> Jesus, treasur'd up all his sayings in my heart;
> but since I have not been able to do that, I will
> labour to live like him, that where he now is, I may
> be also. *And she would often say (as the Prophet* David
> *for his son* Absolon) O that I had dyed for him! *Thus*
> *she continued mourning, till time and conversation had so*
> *moderated her sorrows, that she became the happy Wife*
> *of Sir* Robert Cook of Highnam *in the County of*
> Gloucester *Knight: And though he put a high value*
> *on the excellent accomplishments of her mind and body;*
> *and was so like Mr Herbert, as not to govern like a*

[1] *The Compleat Walton,* 417.   [2] ibid., 413.

> *Master, but as an affectionate Husband; yet she would*
> *even to him often take occasion to mention the name of Mr*
> George Herbert, *and say,* That name must live in
> her memory, till she put off mortality. . . . *Mrs*
> Herbert *was the Wife of Sir* Robert *eight years, and*
> *liv'd his Widow about fifteen; all which time, she took*
> *a pleasure in mentioning, and commending the excellencies*
> *of Mr* George Herbert.[1]

Walton's delight in Mrs Herbert's character and in Sir
Robert Cook's predicament are conveyed without
relaxing a muscle of the sanctimoniousness with which
Herbert's last days have been related. It is passages like
these–and there are several of them–that give a distinguishing flavour to his writings, and when they
directly concern his subjects they add a touch of the
unexpected that prevents easy categorization.

It is difficult to determine how conscious Walton
was in modifying the predominant impression of
character that each of his biographies gives. His theory
of biography as formulated in his prefaces does not go
beyond the commemorative and the pattern. But if his
practice had been perfectly in keeping with his theory,
he would not lie open, particularly in his lives of
Donne and Hooker, to the strictures of Burnet on those
who swell their biographies with trifling accounts of
the private affairs of those persons of whom they
write. Sir Matthew Hale is known to have been none
too comfortably married, but all that Burnet has to
remark is

> I have said little of his Domestick Concerns, since
> though in these he was a great Example; yet it
> signifies nothing to the World, to know any
> particular exercises, that might be given to his
> patience.[2]

Was it Walton's account of Hooker's married life at
which Burnet was glancing? In exemplifying what he

[1] ibid., 451.
[2] *The Life and Death of Sir Matthew Hale* (1682) preface.

believed to have been Hooker's naïveté,[1] in describing what he calls the 'unexpected tempest' of Donne's marriage,[2] and in quoting the rueful punning letter sent by Donne to his wife on being dismissed from Lord Egerton's service – '*John Donne, Anne Donne, Vn-done*'[3] –and in mentioning Donne's wit that was not only able but 'very apt to maintain Paradoxes',[4] in record ing all these things Walton shows a confidence in the truth of what he has discovered and in the peculiarities of the human personality that cannot readily be reduced to the terms of a set character-sketch. In venturing here and there to introduce a discordant note, Walton pays some tribute to the empirical approach. The logic of that approach was to be more clearly demonstrated in the following century.

1962

[1] *The Compleat Walton*, 343.   [2] ibid., 222–3.
[3] ibid., 223.   [4] ibid., 248.

4

The Domestic Manuals of Hannah Wolley

The value of Hannah Wolley's writings cannot be measured in terms of the *Dictionary of National Biography*. Her allotment there is a fraction of a column, ridiculously insufficient for a woman who worked ceaselessly with eminent success 'to testifie to the scandalous World, that I do not altogether spend my time idlely.' 'To be useful in our Generation is partly the intent of our Creation;' she wrote, in the preface to her *Gentlewoman's Companion* in 1675;

> I shall then arrive to the top of the Pyramid of my Contentment, if any shall profit by this following Discourse. . . . The things I pretend greatest skill in, are all works wrought with a Needle, all Transparent works, Shell-work, Moss-work, also cutting of Prints, and adorning Rooms, or Cabinets, or Stands with them.
>
>> All kinds of Beugle-works upon Wyers, or otherwise.
>>
>> All manner of pretty toyes for Closets.
>>
>> Rocks made with Shells, or in Sweets.
>>
>> Frames for Looking glasses, Pictures, or the like.
>>
>> Feathers of Crewel for the corner of Beds.
>>
>> Preserving all kind of Sweet-meats wet and dry.
>>
>> Setting out of Banquets.

Making Salves, Oyntments, Waters, Cordials,
  healing any wounds not desperately
  dangerous.
Knowledg in discerning the Symptomes of
  most Diseases, and giving such remedies as
  are fit in such cases.
All manner of Cookery.
Writing and Arithmetick.
Washing black or white Sarsnets.
Making sweet Powders for the Hair, or to lay
  among Linnen.

Pride of place might have been given to Setting out
of Banquets and All manner of Cookery, since Mrs
Wolley wrote most frequently on those subjects. Her
first publication was *The Ladies Directory, In Choice Experiments & Curiosities of Preserving & Candying both Fruits
and Flowers. Also, An Excellent way of making Cakes, and
other Comfits* [1661]. For this book she was her own pub-
lisher and fixed the price at six shillings, adding 'I
beseech you grudge it not, since there is in it, many
Pounds worth of Skill imparted to you.'

Mrs Wolley addresses her first readers with the
confidence of a practised writer. These are very choice
receipts, she maintains; not taken up on the credit of
others, but commended from her own practice, which
we are to remember from reading her subtitle included
the performance of certain triumphs and trophies of
cookery 'for the Entertainment of his late Majesty, as
well as for the Nobility'. *The Ladies Directory* was
merely a trial volume, she tells us; but if it was 'so well
accepted on, as it was by those who knew both her and
her practice therein' then she would promise to fill
another volume with some of her choicest cookery
'which may be very useful to all that do delight in neat
and noble Entertainments'. Apparently it was, for she
redeemed her promise with her *Cook's Guide* in 1664, her
Exact Cook in 1672, and most amply with her *Queen-like
Closet* published in the same year, a work of such

obvious value that Mrs Wolley's pains were rewarded by a demand for five editions and the apparent fulfilment of her wish not willingly to die while she lived nor to be quite forgotten when she was dead.

Her success had now increased the admired confidence of her address. By her own account she is the acknowledged sovereign of cookery, whose edict is awaited with dutiful impatience. She writes in her *Queen-like Closet*:

> I presume those Bookes which have passed from me formerly, have got me some credit and esteem amongst you. But there being so much time since they were Printed, that me thinks, I hear some of you say *I wish Mrs* Wolley *would put forth some New Experiments*; and to say the Truth, I have been importun'd by divers of my Friends and Acquaintance to do so. . . I do now present you with this *Queen-like Closet*: I do assure you it is worthy of the Title it bears, for the very precious things you will find in it.

¶ The most marked feature of Mrs Wolley's cookery is her avoidance of the commonplace. Hers was truly a royal closet wherein were to be found 'dishes to gratify Noble Persons in their Gusto's'; and therefore though common ingredients could be used they must be disguised or buried under a profusion of spices. This is her recipe for frying Mushrooms:

> Blanch them and wash them clean; if they be large, quarter them, and boil them with Salt, Vinegar, and water, sweet Herbs, large Mace, Cloves, Bay-leaves, and two or three Cloves of Garlick, then take them up, dry them, dip them in butter and fry them in Clarified butter till they be brown; making your sauce for them of Claret-wine, the juice of two or three Oranges, Salt butter, the juice of Horse-radish-root beaten and strained, sliced Nutmeg and Pepper, put these into a

Frying-pan, with the yolks of two or three Eggs,
with some Mutton-Gravy, beat or shake them well
together in the Pan, that they curdle not, then
rub a dish with Garlick, and lay the Mushrooms
therein garnisht with Oranges and Lemons.

Mrs Wolley uses the same profusion of spice to make
Rice Pudding tolerable; she gives directions for boiling
her rice in cream beaten up with the yolks of six eggs,
and seasoned with nutmeg, ginger, cinnamon, pepper,
salt, and sugar. Eggs were poached in the seventeenth
century, but it was thought unseemly that they
should be laid naked upon their bed of toast: they
should first be introduced into a boiling broth of
vinegar and water, flavoured with cloves and mace.
When cooked they should be strewn with currants and
washed in a sauce of verjuice (i.e. crab-apple juice)
butter, and sugar. And how scornfully Mrs Wolley
would have watched our cooks frying sausages in a
little fat: hers were boiled in claret wine with mace and
sweet herbs. She applies the same policy of rich
disguise to the virginal simplicity of lemonade:

Take One Quart of Sack, half a pint of Brandy,
half a Pint of fair Water, the Juice of two Limons,
and some of the Peel, so brew them together
with Sugar, and drink it.

Similarly she knew how to make Pig pass for Lamb,
how Veal could be pickled to eat like Sturgeon, and
Beef or Mutton treated to eat like Venison. This last
was done as follows:

Take your Beef, and dip it in Pigs-blood, or any
new blood, then take Small-beer and Vinegar, and
parboil it therein, let it steep all night, then put
some Turnsole [violet colouring matter] to it;
when it is baked, a good judgment shall not discern
it from Red or Fallow-deer.

Passing from her kickshaws, and leaving aside her
caudles, sillibubs, fricasses, and olios, we find that Mrs
Wolley's principles were modified for the preparation

of her big dishes. Disguise was found to be less necessary and a queen-like luxury of ingredients more
necessary. Behold her making ready to Stew a Pig!
'Take a large Pig to the fire' she writes, and how
effortless it seems; not 'Summon all the maids to help
you carry a large Pig to the fire', not even 'Drag a
large Pig', but 'Take a large Pig' as though it were no
more than a new-born child.

> And when it is hot, skin it, and cut it into
> divers pieces, then take some white wine and
> strong broth, and stew it therein with an
> Onion or two cut very small, a little Pepper, Salt,
> Nutmeg, Thyme, and Anchoves, with some Elder
> Vinegar, sweet Butter and Garie; when it is enough,
> lay Sippets of French Bread in your Dish, and put
> your Meat there on. Garnish your Dish with
> Oranges and Limons.

Her fish recipes are conceived on an equally large scale.
Our herrings, oysters, and anchovies were stuffing
and decorations for her dishes. Pike and Sturgeon for
Hannah. And so,

> Draw a large Pike at the gills; when he is well
> washed, fill the belly with great Oysters, and lard
> the back with pickled herrings; tie it on the spit,
> and baste it with White Wine and Butter, with two
> or three Anchoves dissolved therein; rub your
> dish with garlick, make a sawce with Capers,
> Lemmon, Butter, and White Wine, and some
> Anchoves.'

Her pies must undoubtedly be reckoned among Hannah Wolley's biggest and most interesting dishes.
Upon a pie-crust she laid a good foundation of butter
on which she built Eels and Oysters, or Lampreys, or
Salmon, or Carp, or Steak, or Hares, or Chickens, or
Venison, and to fill in the gaps, carraway seeds, dates,
lemon peel, marrows, currants, cinnamon, pistacho
nuts, eggs, or anything else which she might find in
her capacious larder. The pie could then be baked, but

it was not yet full: the last stage was the cutting open
of the crust to receive a rich draught of wine mixed
with butter, sugar and the yolks of a few eggs. Her
recipe for Chicken Pie will make the process clear:

Make your Paste with cold Cream, Flower,
Butter, the yolk of an Egg, roul it very thin, and
lay it in your Baking-pan, then lay Butter in the
Bottom.

Then lay your Chickens cut in quarters with
some whole Mace, and Nutmeg sliced, with some
Marrow, hard Lettuce, Eryngo Root, and Citron
Pill, with a few Dates stoned and sliced:

Then lay good store of Butter, close up your Pie
and bake it:

Cut it open, put in some Wine, Butter and Sugar,
with the yolks of two or three Eggs well beaten
together over the fire, till it be thick, so serve it to
the Table, and garnish your Dish with some pretty
conceits made in Paste.

¶ At the end of her recipes, Mrs Wolley compiles some
bills of fare for summer and winter dinners. This is her
suggestion for a little family dinner in summer at a
gentleman's house of lesser quality:

First course. 1. a Boiled Pike or Carp stewed;
2. a very fine Pudding boiled; 3. a Chine of Veal,
and another of Mutton; 4. a calves head pie; 5. a
leg of Mutton rosted whole; 6. a couple of Capons,
or a Pig, or a piece of rost Beef, or boiled Beef;
7. a Sallad, the best in season.

These dishes would all be placed on the table at once,
and the diners would endeavour to eat what they could
of each. After the first course, the table was cleared and
the second course served; this consisted of seven more
dishes:

1. a Dish of fat Chickens rosted; 2. a cold Venison
Pasty; 3. a Dish of fryed Pasties; 4. a Joll of Fresh
Salmon; 5. a couple of Lobsters; 6. a dish of Tarts;

> 7. a Gammon of Bacon or Dried Tongues. Then,
> after these are taken away, serve in your
> Cheese and Fruit.

This meal was designed to suit the means of the middle classes; the nobility could afford to provide a more handsome table. Here is Mrs Wolley's bill for a nobleman's Christmas dinner:

> First Course. 1. a Collar of Brawn; 2. a Capon
> and White Broth; 3. a boiled Gurnet; 4. a Dish of
> Boiled Ducks or Rabbits; 5. a rosted Tongue
> and Udder; 6. a made Dish in Puff-Paste; 7. a
> Dish of Scotch Collops of Veal; 8. two Geese in a
> dish; 9. a dish of Capons, two in a dish or three;
> 10. a dish of Set Custards.
>
> Second Course. 1. a young lamb cut in Joints;
> 2. a couple of Fat Rabbits; 3. a Kickshay fryed or
> baked; 4. a Dish of Rosted Mallards; 5. a Leash of
> Partridges; 6. a Pigeon Pie; 7. four Woodcocks in
> a Dish; 8. a dish of Teal, four or six; 9. a cold baked
> Meat; 10. a good Dish of Plover; 11. twelve Snites
> in a Dish; 12. two Dozen of Larks in a Dish; 13.
> another cold baked Meat.
>
> Third Course. 1. an Oyster Pie hot; 2. a Dish
> of fryed Puffes; 3. three or four dried Neats
> Tongues; 4. a Joll of Sturgeon; 5. Laid Tarts in
> Puff Paste; 6. Pickled Oysters; 7. a Dish of Anchovies
> and Caveare; 8. a Quince Pie. When your last
> Course is ended, you must serve in your
> Meat Jellies, your Cheeses of several sorts,
> and your Sweet-Meats.

¶ The reader of Mrs Wolley's Cookery books is not allowed to forget her versatility. Intermingled with receipts are sovereign remedies for the Wind Cholick, for the Griping of the Guts and other digestive affections; and beside these, arrangements were made for selling a most Sovereign Antidote in Powder, where *The Ladies Directory* was sold, as well as excellent Pills,

which had both gained Mrs Wolley 'much Love and
Credit, from those that use them, they being so Safe
and Effectual'. Her remedies are monuments of faith-
healing. Just as in earlier days it was a rule of physick,
the rarer the substance the more cordial; so Mrs
Wolley maintained, the more unusual the more
effectual. Barrows grease, she tells us, if mixed with a
lapful of Archangel leaves makes a sovereign medicine
for any ache or pain; and the patient's hair burnt and
mingled with vinegar and a little pitch will cure forgetfulness. 'Take Sperma Coeti and drink it' she orders
for those troubled with the Red Flux, 'and truss
yourself up with a piece of Black Cotton'. Yet even
when her ingenuity is nauseating, Mrs Wolley never
forgets her humanity: after prescribing a mixture of
apples, paper, and coal grit as a cure for the Bloody
Flux, she is considerate enough to add 'Eat of it, as
your stomach will give leave'. She put most reliance in
every need on the efficacy of her waters. She has *A
Water for the fainting of the Heart, A very good Surfet
Water, An Excellent Water for the Scurvy, A Melancholy
Water, A Water to Whiten the Skin* and one *To make the
Hair fair, A Cordial Orange Water, An Excellent Water for
the Stomach, A Water for the passion of the Heart A most
Precious Water,* and *Walnut Water, or the Water of Life.*
Her most curious alchemy is *Snail Water*, a lengthy and
difficult preparation:

Take a peck of Snailes (with the Houses
on their backs), have in readyness a good fire of
Charcoale well kindled, make a hole in the midst of
the fire, and cast in your snailes, and still renew your
fire till the Snailes be well rosted, then rub them
with a fair cloth, till you have rubbed off all the
green that will come off, then put them in a morter
and bruise them, shells and all; then take Carie,
Celeondine, Burrage, Scabeous, Bugloss, five-leaved
Grass; and if you feel yourself hot, Wood-Sorrel; of
every one of these a good handful, with five tops of

Angelico; these herbs being all bruised in a Morter,
put them in a sweet earthen Pot, with five quarts
of White-Wine, and two quarts of Ale let them steep
all night, then put them into a Limbeck; let the
herbs be in the bottom of the pot, and the Snailes
upon the herbs, and upon the Snailes, put a pint of
Earth-Worms slit, and clean washed; then put upon
them four ounces of Anni-seeds or Fennel-Seeds,
which you please, well bruised, and five great
handfuls of Rose-mary-Flowers well picked, two or
three Races of Turmerick thin sliced, Harts-
horn and Ivory, of each four ounces well steeped
in a quart of White-Wine, till it be like a Jelly,
then put them all in order into the Limbeck, and
draw it forth with care.

In her anxiety to give the correct instructions, Mrs
Wolley has forgotten to disclose its properties.[1]

¶ *The Queen-like Closet* was found indispensable, but Mrs
Wolley was still unsatisfied. She was hag-ridden by
the fear of dying before she could inform her female
readers of all they ought to know. Three laborious
years passed and at length her greatest work, *The
Gentlewoman's Companion*, was ready. She outlines its
scope in the preface. It is to be a '*Universal Companion* and
Guide to the Female Sex, in all *Relations*, *Companies*,
Conditions, and *States* of *Life* even from *Childhood* down
to *Old-age*'. Thirty years of Observation and Experience
had been spent on this work, and three years of writing;
and as she records this, Mrs Wolley thinks with awe of
her task and forestalls the obvious criticism:

I know I may be censured by many for this great
Design, in presenting to all our Sex a compleat
Directory, and that which contains several Sciences:
deeming it a Work for a *Solomon*, who could give

[1] *The Queen-like Closet* (1675) 17–18, makes it clear, however,
that snail water is 'excellent for Consumptions'. Cp. 306–7 for
a simpler recipe.

an account from the Cedar to the Hysop; [yet] I
must tell them, I look upon the end of Life to be
Usefulness; nor know I wherein our Sex can be
more useful in their Generation then having a
competent skill in Physick and Chirurgery, a
competent Estate to distribute it, and a Heart
willing thereunto.

Besides giving instruction in the useful crafts of
Physick, Cookery, Needle-Work, and the washing of
Black and White Sarsnets, Mrs Wolley suggests a plan
of more cultural education for her readers. They should
study some practical books of Divinity, but at the
same time they must not neglect the Romances such
as *Cassandra*, *The Grand Cyrus*, and Sir Philip Sidney's
Arcadia, all of which 'treat of Generosity, Gallantry,
and Virtue'. They must learn Latin and Italian, paying
special attention to Latin, which will enable them to
speak true and good English, and be freed 'from the
fear of recountring such who make it their business to
ransack a new World of words to find out what are
long and obscure', 'Fops of Rhetorick' as she indig-
nantly calls these creatures, 'spawns of non-intelligency',
who will 'venture the spraining of their tongues, and
splay-footing their own mouths, if they can but cramp
a Young Gentlewoman's intellect'.

Mrs Wolley deserves to be remembered if only
because she was an early feminist, fighting what must
have seemed to her a losing battle in that unenlightened
age for the recognition of female intelligence. As she
rises to the height of her great argument her prose
becomes more and more ornate, even euphuism is
employed to strengthen her position:

Vain man is apt to think we were meerly intended for the World's propagation, and to keep
its humane inhabitants sweet and clean; but by
their leaves, had we the same Literature, they would
find our brains as fruitful as our bodies. Hence I
am induced to believe, we are debarred from the

> knowledge of humane learning, lest our pregnant
> Wits should rival the towering conceits of our in-
> sulting Lords and Masters.

And pretending to reluct at the excess of her passion, she continues:

> Pardon the Severity of this expression, since I
> intend not thereby to infuse bitter Rebellion into
> the sweet blood of Females; for know, I would
> have all such as are enter'd into the honourable
> state of Matrimony to be loyal and loving Subjects
> to their lawful (though lording) Husbands. I cannot
> but complain of, and must condemn the great
> negligence of Parents, in letting the fertile ground
> of their Daughters lie fallow, yet send the barren
> Noddles of their sons to the University, where
> they stay for no other purpose than to fill their
> empty Sconces with idle notions to make a noise
> in the Country.

Mrs Wolley knows as much about manners as she does about cookery. She was not a schoolmaster's wife for nothing. Her chapters 'Of the Gait or Gesture' and 'Of the Government of the Eye' might still be read with profit by a débutante; and her letter-writer is as nearly complete as any Restoration lady could desire. There is a letter from one lady to another condemning artificial beauty, with the ingenious lady's reply, a letter from a mother persuading her daughter from wearing Spots and Black-patches on her face, with the dutiful daughter's defence, and a letter of Love Protested with an answer of Love Repuls'd. Forms of congratulation are arranged, and instruction given on more difficult points such as 'How to complain elegantly of injuries done' and 'How to set about a dear female-friend whom you suspect of any youthful excursions'.

¶ But Mrs Wolley is happiest when she has a meal in sight. Having given directions for arranging a bill of fare and cooking the dishes, she has still to superintend the service. Those who wait at table are instructed not to hold the plates before their mouths for fear they should defile them with their breath, nor to eat the remains of the courses as they carry them to the kitchen. All is not yet complete. Mrs Wolley is so fastidious that she could not enjoy her dinner unless her guests behaved fittingly. She therefore issued the following directions:

> Wipe your spoon every time you put it into the
> [main] dish; otherwise you may offend some
> squeamish stomacks. Eat not so fast, though
> very hungry, as by gormandizing you are ready
> to choak your selves. Close your lips when you
> eat; talk not when you have meat in your mouth;
> and do not smack like a Pig, nor make any other
> noise which shall prove ungrateful to the com-
> pany. If your pottage be so hot your mouth cannot
> endure it, have patience till it be of a fit coolness;
> for it is very unseemly to blow it in your spoon,
> or otherwise. . . It is very uncomely to drink so
> large a draught, that your breath is almost gone,
> and are forced to blow strongly to recover yourself:
> nor let it go down too hastily, lest it force you
> to an extreme cough, or bring it up again, which
> would be a great rudeness to nauseate the whole
> Table.

And now her work is finished. The Table is set, ser-vants and guests know their parts, the wine and sugar are luxuriating the pie, the cheeses and sweet-meats are in order on the tray, and Mrs Wolley has leisure to compose some valedictory couplets:

> Ladies, I hope your pleas'd, and so shall I
> If what I've writ, you may be gainers by:
> If not; it is your fault, it is not mine,
> Your benefit in this I do design.
> Much labour and much time it hath me cost,

Therefore I beg, let none of it be lost.
The Mony you shall pay for this my Book,
You'l not repent of, when in it you look.
No more at present to you I shall say,
But wish you all the happiness I may.

1931

The Imitation of Horace in English Poetry

My subject is the imitation of Horace by certain English poets, not the translation of Horace; or rather, not exclusively translation, for by imitation I mean something of wider significance. I mean to consider some of the work of three English poets, each of whom had studied Horace and enjoyed his study, show what they borrowed from Horace, and what they made of their borrowing.

I have chosen three poets whose imitations were made with different purposes in view. What Pope borrowed from Horace was Horace's words: what Milton imitated was Horace's technique, and what Herrick imitated – spasmodically – was the Horatian view of life. I shall qualify that somewhat too dogmatic statement in what follows, but it will serve to indicate the chief interest of each borrower.

Borrowing Horace's words has been done with various intentions. At its lowest, the borrowing has been done to provide short cuts for schoolboys. Or it has been done to help the reader who is ignorant of Latin to what must necessarily be some faint appreciation of Horace's genius and to some understanding of what he teaches. That was the intention of Creech in the seventeenth century, Francis in the eighteenth, and Conington in the nineteenth.

Or it has been done to indicate a parallel between

contemporary conditions of life and conditions in classical times. For this purpose it is a device of peculiar value to the satirist, the panegyrist, and the critic. If the sins of, say, eighteenth-century London bear some superficial resemblance to the sins of Imperial Rome, the authority of the modern satirist is greatly enhanced if he can put on the mantle of Juvenal, and suggest by imitating Juvenal's Third Satire, paragraph by paragraph (as Dr Johnson did in his poem *London*) that it is in just that manner that the great Roman satirist would have attacked London society if he had been living in the eighteenth century. Or the panegyrist can convey an ingenious compliment to a patron or a friend if he can produce modern parallels for the phrases of an ode or epistle of Horace addressed to Maecenas or Ofellus. Lastly the critic can invoke the authority and prestige of standards some two thousand years old by adapting the *Ars Poetica* to modern conditions, as Byron did in his *Hints from Horace*, and as Oldham had done long before him.

This manner of translation was known as imitating, and became a favourite poetic form both in England and France between 1660 and 1750. It sprang readily enough from the ideals of spirited translation current at that time. The literalness of such work as Ben Jonson's version of the *Ars Poetica* was beginning to be disparaged—it was neither Latin nor English, people felt—and, instead, translators attempted to make their author 'speak such English as he would himself have spoken, if he had been born in England, and in this present age'.[1] The words are Dryden's, who was one of the most eminent practitioners of this spirited translation, which is at times indistinguishable from imitation and led directly to it. What it meant in practice was that when Dryden found Ovid writing in the *Ars Amatoria*, 'if you want girls, do your hunting

[1] Dedication of the *Aeneis. Essays of John Dryden*, ed. W. P. Ker (Oxford 1926) II, 228.

especially in the round theatres *sed tu praecipue curvis venare theatris*', he rendered the passage

> But above all, the Play-House is the Place;
> There's Choice of Quarry in that narrow Chace.[1]

or in one of the *Amores*, 'the letters which a dexterous maidservant brings backwards and forwards (between your wife and her lover)' (*Quas ferat et referat sollers ancilla tabellas*), he renders

> An Orange-wench wou'd tempt thy Wife abroad,
> Kick her, for she's a Letter-bearing Bawd.[2]

It is in this well-established tradition that we find Pope working too.

It is clear to him that if Horace had lived in eighteenth-century England, he would have retired from town not, of course, to a Sabine farm, but to a country villa at Twickenham, and his patron would have been not Maecenas but Bolingbroke. And if Horace had composed the first Ode of the fourth book in the 1730s he would not have written *Non sum Qualis eram bonae Sub regno Cynarae* but

> I am not now, alas! the man
> As in the gentle Reign of My Queen *Anne*:[3]

or instead of dreaming in that ode that he was pursuing Ligurina across the Campus Martius, he would have seen Martha Blount 'swiftly shoot along the Mall, Or softly glide by the Canal'.[4]

Pope imitated Horace only because it suited his immediate purpose. He did not set out to modernize the satires as he set out with the purpose of translating Homer. It was much more accidental than that. The first *Imitation* was written in the latter part of January

---

[1] *Ovid's Art of Love*, 98–9. Cp. *Ars amatoria*, I, 89.
[2] 'Several of Ovid's Elegies, Book II. Elegy the Nineteenth', 41–2. Cp. *Amores*, II, xix, 41.
[3] *Imitations of Horace*, Od. IV, i, 3–4.
[4] op. cit., 45–6.

1733, when Pope was confined to his room with a fever. One of his visitors was Bolingbroke, who happened to take up a Horace which lay on Pope's table, and in turning over the leaves, chanced upon the first satire of the second book. 'He observed,' said Pope, relating the incident to his friend, Spence, 'how well that would hit my case, if I were to imitate it in English. After he was gone, I read it over, translated it in a morning or two, and sent it to the press in a week or fortnight after. And this was the occasion of my imitating some other of the Satires and Epistles afterwards.'[1]

Horace's poem is an introduction to the satires which follow, and is an apology for writing satire. The reason why this poem hit Pope's case was that he was still alarmed by the outcry on his *Epistle to Lord Burlington* which had been published just over a year earlier. The satirical character of *Timon* in that poem had been angrily proclaimed as a portrait of the Duke of Chandos, and though Pope denied it he was not believed. The clamour made him anxious for the reception of another poem, the *Epistle to Lord Bathurst*, on which he had been at work for some time and which had been published shortly before the *Imitation of Horace*. It is quite clear that the *Imitation* was intended as a rearguard to both of these larger and more important poems.

I mention the history of the composition and publication of the first *Imitation of Horace* to emphasize how unusual its occasion was. One might well imagine that it would have been much simpler for Pope to write an original work if he needed to defend himself and his two poems from certain specific charges. But instead he preferred to invoke the authority of Horace, or if you prefer it, to tie himself hand and foot by translating a poem of Horace for this purpose. In the circumstances one would expect no translation at all, but if a translation, then certainly a very loose one. The astonishing

[1] J. Spence *Observations, Anecdotes, and Characters*, ed. J. M. Osborn (Oxford 1966) I, 143.

thing is that Pope translates or imitates religiously, phrase by phrase, producing modern parallels for Horace's allusions, and not omitting above four short passages from the original. Moreover, the result was not a mere academic exercise; Pope's defence was so lively that it evoked a crude retort in what might be considered very poor taste from his enemy, Lady Mary Wortley Montagu.

Pope's imitation would not be of much use as a crib, though on at least one occasion he has produced a good solution of that kind of difficulty which continually recurs in translation, when a word in the original bears two meanings and the sense requires the secondary meaning as well as the primary. Horace says that he is not going to use his *stylus* to attack all and sundry unprovoked. *Stylus* means a *dagger* and a *pen*, and Horace intends both meanings. What can we do in English, where we have no single word for this double service? Pope solves the difficulty very prettily:

> Satire's my Weapon, but I'm too discreet
> To run a Muck, and tilt at all I meet.[1]

But even such a short passage as that distinguishes Pope from Horace. One could imagine Horace using the Latin equivalent of *discreet*, even the Latin equivalent of *run a Muck* (whatever that is; though I imagine it is not the colourless *petit* which Horace does use here); but it would be difficult to imagine Horace using the equivalent of such a significant word as *tilt*. My point is that throughout his *Imitation*, Pope is eager to enrich Horace's expression.

The following passage gives a better, though still a slight, example. Horace finds that this weapon, this *stylus*, even when it is in its sheath, protects him by its mere presence; so, he continues, why should I bother to draw it when I am *safe from dangerous robbers*? Horace is merely continuing the metaphor. He adds nothing

[1] *Imitations of Horace*, Sat. II, i, 69–70.

to the previous passage by the generality *Tutus ab infestis latronibus*.[1] But Pope cannot resist the chance of particularizing. He takes the opportunity of enumerating some of the enemies from whom he is preserved—not personal enemies, but enemies of every virtuous Englishman:

> Satire's my Weapon, but I'm too discreet
> To run a Muck, and tilt at all I meet;
> I only wear it in a Land of Hectors,
> Thieves, Supercargoes, Sharpers, and Directors.

The Hectors were first cousins to the Mohawks, irresponsible young bloods who bullied anyone they met in the streets of London; and the Directors, as always in the literature of this period, were the infamous Directors of the South Sea Company.

Horace continues by maintaining that he is a peace-loving fellow: 'but he who provokes me—*commorit*—(better not touch me, I cry,) will weep for it and be well known in song—*insignis cantabitur*—throughout the whole city.'[2] Once more, one notices in Pope's rendering an enrichment of Horace's words; and incidentally, Pope seizes the chance of paying a compliment to the French Prime Minister, and of reflecting on Walpole's Whig government with which he was not in sympathy:

>   *at ille,*
> *Qui me commorit (melius non tangere clamo)*
> *Flebit, et insignis tota cantabitur urbe*

> Peace is my dear Delight—not *Fleury's* more;
> But touch me, and no Minister so sore.
> Who-e'er offends, at some unlucky Time
> Slides into Verse, and hitches in a Rhyme,
> Sacred to Ridicule! his whole Life long,
> And the sad Burthen of some merry Song.[3]

[1] Sat. II, i, 42.
[2] Sat. II, i, 44–6.
[3] *Imitations of Horace*, Sat. II, i, 75–80.

Those parenthetic thrusts and compliments are a constant source of delight to those who compare Pope with his original. 'Some say', writes Horace, 'that verses like mine can be spun (*deduci*) at the rate of a thousand a day.' And Pope, glad of an opportunity to attack the effeminate Lord Hervey:

> The lines are weak, another's pleas'd to say,
> Lord *Fanny* spins a thousand such a Day.[1]

Or, asks Horace, in reference to Augustus's victories, 'How can such a one as I describe the Wounds of the Parthian falling from his horse?' This reminded Pope of an absurd poem by Budgell describing the heroic death of George II's charger, so he asks whether he is expected to emulate '*Budgell*'s Fire and Force,' and 'Paint Angels trembling round his *falling Horse*.'[2] Perhaps the parallel is a little strained; he was more lucky in being able to reflect on the Government's policy of keeping a large standing army in time of peace with the lines

> Save but our *Army*! and let *Jove* incrust
> Swords, Pikes, and Guns, with everlasting Rust![3]

when Horace had written the merely pious invocation

> *O pater et rex*
> *Juppiter, ut pereat positum rubigine telum.*[4]

But it is comparatively little that Pope owes to luck. The inexhaustible stock of witty parallels, the clever renderings, Horace's compliments to Augustus ironically inverted into sarcasm at the expense of George II, are the work of genius.

With this one must reckon the constant enrichment of Horace's language, and all of this not in one poem only, but in the whole series of *Imitations*. They are not altogether Horatian, of course; Horace chooses Ofellus's

[1] op. cit., 5–6.   [2] op. cit., 27–8.   [3] op. cit., 73–4.
[4] Sat. II, i, 42–3.

simple way of life to praise, Pope prefers to praise his own; Horace, more frequently than Pope, spares the name when he lashes the vice; and Pope knew quite well that he was not following Horace's principles. In the first Dialogue of the *Epilogue to the Satires* he puts the observation into the mouth of his friend–who commends Horace for understatement:

> But *Horace*, Sir, was delicate, was nice;
> *Bubo* observes, he lash'd no sort of *Vice*:
> Horace would say, *Sir* Billy *serv'd the Crown*,
> Blunt[1] could *do bus'ness*, Huggins[2] *knew the Town*:
> In *Sappho* touch the *Failing of the Sex*,
> In rev'rend Bishops note some *small Neglects*,
> And own, the *Spaniard* did a *waggish thing*,
> Who cropt our Ears, and sent them to the King.
> His sly, polite, insinuating stile
> Could please at Court, and make A U G U S T U S smile:
> An artful Manager, that crept between
> His Friend and Shame, and was a kind of *Screen*.[3]

But that was not Pope's method. He preferred to

> Brand the bold Front of shameless guilty Men,
> Dash the proud Gamester in his gilded Car,

and (one of the best lines he ever wrote)

> Bare the mean Heart that lurks beneath a Star.[4]

This is a different ideal; and I suggest that when we read Pope's *Imitations of Horace*, what we should admire is the virtuosity of his treatment of the Latin, his ability to divert Horace's words into different intentions, and to load every rift with Popian ore–I suggest we should admire all this instead of condemning him,

[1] Director of the South Sea Company.

[2] John Huggins was Warden of the Fleet prison. He was tried in 1729 for the murder of one of his prisoners, and was acquitted. During the trial he called 'vast numbers of gentlemen of the first quality' to witness to his blameless life.

[3] *Epilogue to the Satires*, Dia. I, 11–22.

[4] *Imitations of Horace*, Sat. II, i, 106–8.

as some have done, for not subduing his personality and attempting to become another Horace.

¶ In considering the imitations of Horace's technique, it would be possible once more to examine Pope at length. In such poems as *The Epistle to Dr Arbuthnot* and the *Epilogue to the Satires* he has succeeded in imitating the 'talking' verse of Horace's satires, with its occasional breaking up of the hexameter for the purpose of repartee or brisk conversational exchanges. And like Horace, Pope often leaves these conversational levels to rise to a more rhetorical height when contemplating some virtuous action. It may be useful, however, to turn to the Odes.

Perhaps the most interesting attempt which an English poet has made to learn something from the technique of the Odes is Milton's. So far as we know he only once tried his hand at translating an ode; the ode he chose being the fifth of the first book, the *Quis multa gracilis*. His purpose was to translate word for word, as far as possible, and at the same time to retain something of the Latin measure. Now, in the previous generation of English poets, there had been considerable discussion on the desirability of writing English poetry in Latin verse forms. Spenser had toyed with the notion, and Campion had defended it; but in the end contemporary practice and the logic of Daniel's criticism had defeated the Latinists. The use of rhyme was also involved in the controversy; those who championed classical metres decried rhyme, those who held to accentual rhythms allowed it. Now Milton belonged to both sides: he disapproved of classical metres for English poetry, and as he grew older he disapproved more and more of rhyme. This of course affects his translation of Horace's ode. He cannot adopt the Latin metre, because English poetry is written according to its own accentual rhythms; but he follows the Latin Alcaic in making the last two lines of each verse shorter than the first two, and he admits no rhyme.

This, then, is his verse-form:

What slender Youth bedew'd with liquid odours
Courts thee on Roses in some pleasant Cave,
    Pyrrha for whom bind'st thou
    In wreaths thy golden Hair.[1]

But that is by no means the full extent of Milton's imitation. One of the characteristics of the Latin ode is the emphasis put upon certain words and phrases by holding them over until they can be given an important position either in a later line or in the next verse. For example, the first verse ends with *cui flavam religas comam*, leaving *simplex munditiis* for the important position at the beginning of the next. In the third verse there are two examples:

Qui nunc te fruitur credulus aurea:
Qui semper vacuam, semper amabilem
    Sperat, nescius aurae
    Fallacis. *Miseri, quibus*
Intentata nites.

the last two words being the first two of the next verse. The effect of this is to produce a cross rhythm: while we are observing the ordained rhythm of the verse, the importance of these words and phrases forces us to set up another rhythm in order to preserve the sense. This cross-rhythm is more frequently met with in music, where quavers in one part struggle against triplets in another, or when, in songs, the vocal line is broken by a rest in the music where there is no pause in the sense of the words. It is quite easy in music to maintain both rhythms, or to sing through a rest (as it is called) and it should be possible to produce the same effect in reading verse. Milton, noticing the cross rhythms in Horace, attempts to preserve them in his translation;

[1] *Poetical Works*, ed. H. Darbishire (Oxford 1952–5) II, 158.

but in my opinion they are more obvious to the eye than to the ear:

> What slender Youth, bedew'd with liquid odours,
> Courts thee on Roses in some pleasant Cave,
> > *Pyrrha* for whom bind'st thou
> > In wreaths thy golden Hair,
> Plain in thy neatness; O how oft shall he
> On Faith and changed Gods complain: and Seas
> > Rough with black winds and storms
> > Unwonted shall admire:
> Who now enjoyes thee credulous, all Gold,
> Who alwayes vacant, alwayes amiable,
> > Hopes thee; of flattering gales
> > Unmindfull. Hapless they
> To whom thou untry'd seem'st fair. Me in my
> > vow'd
> Picture the sacred wall declares t' have hung
> > My dank and dropping weeds
> > To the stern God of Sea.

'Plain in thy neatness' and 'of flattering gales Unmindful' are well preserved, but I am doubtful about the others: 'To whom thou untry'd seem'st fair' cannot compare either in emphasis or in concision with *intentata nites*.

A further characteristic of this and other odes is that they have not yielded their full meaning when one has merely established the sense of the words and their grammatical relationships. There are what one might call harmonics of meaning in the relative position of words, that is to say, in their neighbourhood one with another. For example, one observes in the first verse that *puer* is the subject, *urget* the verb, *te* the object, and that *perfusus liquidis odoribus* depends upon *puer*—a slender youth, bedewed with liquid odours, is courting thee. But surely there is an alliance between *urget* and *odoribus*—*perfusus liquidis urget odoribus*. Surely Horace is suggesting without actually saying so, that the liquid

odours are playing a great part in the success of the
courtship–that Pyrrha is delighted at their scent.
Horace can convey this secondary meaning without
disturbing the primary meaning because Latin is an
inflected language and therefore does not entirely
depend upon word-order for making the primary sense
clear. But English is uninflected and it must pay the
penalty; the subsidiary meaning cannot be suggested
so neatly. Milton had an ear for these Horatian harmonics but he found it almost impossible to reproduce
them. 'What slender Youth bedew'd with liquid odours
Courts thee'; the harmonic is lost, or very nearly. He
was a little more successful in the third verse: *Qui nunc
te fruitur credulus aurea.* In addition to the primary
meaning of *credulus aurea*, I think we can hear Horace
warning the lad that 'All is not gold that glitters'.
Milton recognized the importance of the juxtaposition,
but all he could manage by way of rendering it was
'Who now enjoyes thee credulous, all Gold'.

Some of these experiments in mastering Horace's
technique Milton adopted in his sonnets. It was Robert
Bridges who first drew attention to the similarity between Milton's sonnets and Horace's odes. Horace used
the ode as an occasional poem–he wrote one when a
wolf fled from him on his Sabine estate; Milton made a
similar use of the sonnet. Horace's invitations to eat
and drink are in ode form, Milton's are in sonnet form;
Horace uses the ode to address politicians and express
his political convictions, and that exactly describes
Milton's sonnets to Cromwell, Vane and Fairfax;
lastly, some of Horace's odes are characterized by
abrupt transitions from one topic to another, and if the
briefness of the sonnet does not allow Milton to do the
same, it pleases him occasionally to contrast the subject
or mood of the octave with that of the sestet, as in the
sonnets to Cromwell, Fairfax, Lawrence and Lady
Margaret Ley. But in addition to the similarity of
purpose, Milton's sonnets bear some relation to the

Odes in technique, as well. Milton's fondness for cross rhythms, his dislike of sense and verse pausing together, is as evident as Horace's; and though the sonnet form compels him to use a rhyme scheme, he chooses the Italian form rather than the Shakespearian. The reason for this choice was that he regarded himself as an Italian sonneteer writing in English; but he may also have reflected that the rhymes in the sestet of the Italian sonnet are not nearly so insistent to the ear as the rhymes in the sestet of the Shakespearian; and the Italian sonnet avoids the rhyming couplet which concludes and clinches the Shakespearian. The sonnet to Lawrence is a good example of Milton at his most Horatian (and incidentally the force of its concluding couplet is subdued by the absence of rhyme):

> *Lawrence* of vertuous Father vertuous Son,
>> Now that the Fields are dank, and ways are mire,
>> Where shall we sometimes meet, and by the fire
>> Help wast a sullen day; what may be won
> From the hard Season gaining: time will run
>> On smoother, till *Favonius* re-inspire
>> The frozen earth; and cloath in fresh attire
>> The Lillie and Rose, that neither sow'd nor spun.
> What neat repast shall feast us, light and choice,
>> Of Attick tast, with Wine, whence we may rise
>> To hear the Lute well toucht, or artfull voice
> Warble immortal Notes and *Tuskan* Ayre?
>> He who of those delights can judge, and spare
>> To interpose them oft, is not unwise.[1]

That is as near as we can expect to approach to Horace's mood and Horace's methods in verse, and it must surely be admitted that the approach was made easier by Milton choosing such an uncontroversial subject as an invitation to spend a day in the country. Even so, Milton's invitations were more austere than those of Horace. It is true that Horace, in his invitations,

[1] *Poetical Works*, II, 155.

is apt to refer discomfortingly to cypresses and to the inevitability of fretful old age, but there is always recompense in store. Lawrence, on the other hand, must have known quite well that there was no chance of a *gratus puellæ risus ab angulo* or a *pignus dereptum* if he visited Milton. And the differences in mood become more apparent still when we compare Milton's political sonnets and Horace's political odes. We are driven to the obvious conclusion that Milton, like Pope, borrowed from Horace just so much as would suit his purpose, and no more.

¶ One must look elsewhere, then, for a consistent effort to imitate Horace's temperament and philosophy, and not delay over these invitations of Milton's in the manner of *O Saepe Mecum* or over the meditations of Campion and Sir Henry Wotton on the theme of *Integer Vitae*, or even–and this is a greater temptation– over Shirley's grand success in maintaining the majestic music of the last two verses of *Aequam memento*. Shirley's lyric, *The glories of our blood and state*, is the exact counter- part of *Divesne prisco natus ab Inacho*; Horace and Shirley have met here, but their paths soon diverge again. All these are transitory likenesses; but there is at any rate one poet whose resemblance to Horace it is worth examining more closely, and that is Herrick; for their resemblance is not one of mere casual imitation.

Herrick knew his Horace well. He had had a classical education at Cambridge, and later enjoyed the company of Ben Jonson, which probably stood him in better stead, for no one at that time appreciated the Latin lyric writers more than Jonson did. Like Horace, Herrick had moved in court circles and had made his bid to be considered an unofficial poet laureate. Then, later, like Horace, he knew the pleasures of country retirement. Like Horace, his loves are numerous but not disturbing, and, like Horace again, he frequently imagines himself in the part of the middle-aged lover.

His appreciation of good wine was as acute as Horace's, and his praise of the simple life as sincere. Each poet, too, was convinced of his immortality, and just as Horace writes an *Exegi monumentum* for the conclusion of the third book of the odes, so Herrick erects a pillar of fame for the conclusion of the *Hesperides*:

> Fames pillar here, at last, we set,
> Out-during *Marble*, *Brasse*, or *Jet*,
>   Charm'd and enchanted so,
>   As to withstand the blow
>   Of overthrow:
>   Nor shall the seas,
>   Or Outrages
>   of Storms orebear
>   What we up-rear;
>   Tho Kingdoms fal,
> This pillar never shall
> Decline or waste at all;
> But stand for ever by his owne
> Firm and well fixt foundation.[1]

But Herrick especially appreciated Horace's seriousness. The famous *Gather ye rosebuds* and *To Daffodils* are not light-hearted advice for enjoying the present smiling hour and letting tomorrow take care of itself. They suggest, as Horace also suggests, the ominous future which may be in store for us. Herrick is fond of preaching this sober epicureanism, and like Horace he continually warns us not to be softened by good fortune:

> Adversity hurts none, but onely such
> Whom whitest Fortune dandled has too much.[2]

And how Horatian is such a poem as this, entitled *Men mind no state in sickness*:

[1] *Poetical Works*, ed. L. C. Martin (Oxford 1956) 335.
[2] op. cit., 239.

That flow of Gallants which approach
To kisse thy hand from out the coach;
That fleet of Lackeyes, which do run
Before thy swift Postilion;
Those strong-hoof'd Mules, which we behold,
Rein'd in with Purple, Pearl, and gold,
And shod with silver, prove to be
The drawers of the *axeltree.*
Thy Wife, thy Children, and the State
of *Persian* Loomes, and *antique* Plate:
And these, and more, shall then afford
No joy to thee their sickly Lord.[1]

One might suppose that the English Horace was found
at last. But it is not so; and if one begins to consider
the differences between Horace and Herrick and to try
to account for them, one would do well to pay attention
to what at first glance may appear trivial: Horace's
Sabine farm, was little more than thirty miles from
Rome, whereas Dean Prior, Herrick's vicarage, is nearly
200 miles from London. Horace could easily return
to Rome, and his friends could easily visit him in the
country; there was no danger of his becoming pro-
vincial; but that is just what did happen to Herrick
because of his enforced and remote seclusion. His dis-
similarity from Horace is largely owing to his eccentricity, his mixing of epigrams with dirges, and his
readiness to prattle whatever the occasion, and his
accounts of personal behaviour (which sounds odd for
a country dweller). Following Horace he offers little
sacrifices to Lar, propitiates his household gods, pays
deference to Roman religious observances. These
things are right in Horace because they were part of his
own cultural background and the cultural background
of his readers. But Herrick, far away from his cultural
equals, resurrects in the seclusion of Devonshire a
pagan culture which had been dead many hundreds

[1] ibid.

of years and bore no relation to life in seventeenth-century England. This is what people mean when they call Herrick's poetry quaint. It is not the poetry of a man of the world like Horace. We are thus driven to the paradoxical conclusion that by following Horace too closely in this Herrick became un-Horatian.

But supposing Herrick's country retreat had been in Surrey, and suppose he could have commanded the broad, sweeping tones of *Aequam memento rebus in arduis*, which he never attempts–his music is of slighter build–would he have wanted to make himself a second Horace? There is evidence to suggest that he would not. One of Herrick's most remarkable characteristics is the range of his poetic moods and the ease and rapidity with which he can give the appearance of shifting from one to another. I say 'can give the appearance of shifting', for it is because his verse is largely epigrammatic that we gain this impression. And with a large quantity of epigrams to arrange into a volume of verse, Herrick had, and took, the opportunity of presenting some contrasts of mood and address which are both pleasing and piquant. Several poets might have written both a welcome for King Charles on leading his army into the West, and an epigram on the roses on Julia's bosom: only Herrick would think of placing the two poems side by side. Some of Herrick's contemporaries might have offered prayers both to Venus and to the Christian God: none but Herrick would have used identical verse forms and turns of expression as though to draw attention to his divided allegiance. He takes great pains to show his readers that he is a creature of moods to none of which he will give exclusive attention. The same is true of his devotion to the ancient poets. For the most part, his love-making is deliciously frivolous; but at times, as in such a poem as *To Anthea*, he can almost make us believe that he has the passion of Catullus. And when he has been warning us in all sincerity to observe an *aurea mediocritas*, we find him soon after arm in arm with Anacreon, each of them besmeared with grapes, wearing coronets of roses, and declaring that they are ready to drink the aged Caecuban until the roof turns round. I think he was most faithful to the Cyrenaic philosophy. His business was to experience each moment as intensely as possible–to realize, as he pressed Julia's lips, that her soul and love were *palpable* in this, or to swoon with delight at the tempestuousness of her petticoat; to be all Anacreon one day, to be all Horace the next, and to lead the life of an Anglican clergyman on the third. Clearly, then, Horace governed only a part, though an important part, of Herrick's temperament. Like Pope and Milton, Herrick borrowed from Horace, but not exclusively, and what he borrowed he used for the fulfilment of his own poetic purpose.

These three men are typical of the best English disciples of Horace. They come to him to learn, not to mimic–though Herrick sometimes made that mistake –and having taken from him what they needed, they went their own way.

1939

Science and Man in Eighteenth-Century Poetry

I suppose that most twentieth-century students find
themselves more at home in the seventeenth century
than in the eighteenth. The mental equipment of a
well-educated seventeenth-century Englishman was
very different from that of his modern descendant, but
the problems he had to deal with are oddly familiar.
Like him, we know what it means to live in a world of
political unrest, continually under the shadow of war.
We too can see what effect this unrest has upon moral
codes, upon the whole domestic scene. We too can echo
his exclamation as he surveyed the state of the world:

> 'Tis all in peeces, all cohaerence gone;
> All just supply, and all Relation.[1]

And to mention something which particularly affects
us university teachers, we, from our twentieth-
century experience, can readily sympathize with
Thomas Fuller, seizing a few intervals from his duties
as chaplain to Hopton's army in the west to collect
material for his *Worthies of England*, or with that great
non-juror, George Hickes, who, like some of our
continental colleagues, was pursued for nine years
from one hiding place to another, and yet managed to
produce that *Thesaurus* of his which still remains our

[1] Donne *An Anatomie of the World* (1611) 213f.

standard treasury of knowledge about Saxon antiquities.[1]

The troubles of our seventeenth-century ancestors are indeed familiar to men of our generation, more familiar to *us* than to the men of the eighteenth and nineteenth centuries. And most familiar of all is the trouble to which they were put in assimilating the results of scientific discovery. We can detect at least three important aspects of this problem in the minds of seventeenth-century writers. First, there was the problem of using this newly discovered knowledge for the relief of man's estate. That was in the front of Bacon's mind as he wrote both *The Advancement of Learning* and the *New Atlantis*; for though he was prepared to justify scientific studies as complementary to the study of divinity, the one being a study of God's words and the other a study of His works, yet Bacon's interest quickens noticeably when his theme permits him to pass from the value of pure science to the value of applied, and to prophesy the marvels with which scientists would gratify us in years to come: aeroplanes, telephones, submarines, artificial silk, synthetic diamonds, synthetic food, and synthetic wine.

Secondly, there was the problem of reconciling the new learning with old traditions. Must we abandon our most cherished beliefs, it was asked, if their scientific foundation is now proved to be inadequate? Has the Bible and all it teaches us been affected by these discoveries? Where does the frontier lie between what sense and reason tell us and what we hold as a matter of faith? This was a problem which exercised all the best minds of the day. At the beginning of the century we find Bacon composing a prayer for scientists to repeat:

[1] 'The investigations which were later to produce the most elaborate treatise of historical philology that was ever devoted to the Anglo-Saxon language were carried on by a political refugee busy with the constant preparation of pamphlets and risking his neck in negotiations with a deposed prince'. D. C. Douglas *English Scholars* (1939) 100.

This also we humbly and earnestly beg, that Human
things may not prejudice such as are Divine; neither
that from the unlocking of the gates of sense,
and the kindling of a greater natural light, anything of incredulity or intellectual night may arise
in our minds towards the Divine Mysteries. But
rather that by our mind throughly cleansed and
purged from fancy and vanities, and yet subject and
perfectly given up to the Divine Oracles, there may
be given unto Faith the things that are Faith's.[1]

Some eighty years later the relationship of reason and
faith, of what science and of what the Bible teaches us,
looked a little clearer. The scientists had not become
atheistical after all. Some most eminent divines of the
Church of England had assisted in bringing the Royal
Society to birth, and a future Bishop was the young
Society's first historian; while the greatest of all English
scientists was widely believed to be a devout Christian.
Newton's faith, at any rate, seemed undisturbed by his
scientific studies, and Locke could confidently define
the limits of what had been supposed to be warring
mental faculties:

Faith is nothing but a firm assent of the mind:
which if it be regulated, as is our duty, cannot be
afforded to any thing but upon good reason; and
so cannot be opposite to it.[2]

Thus science might be justified in its purpose or by its
fruits; rightly understood it could not contribute to
infidelity, and was indeed more likely to enlarge our
knowledge of God in the contemplation of his works.

There was, also, one further question which
perplexed the minds of seventeenth-century English-
men as they attempted to assimilate this new experience. If science can do so much for man, ought we all
to be engaged in pursuing it, as the inhabitants of
Bacon's New Atlantis were? It is, no doubt, the proper

[1] Bacon *Works*, ed. J. Spedding, etc, (1857–74) VII, 259.
[2] *An Essay concerning Human Understanding*, IV, xvii, 24.

study of some men; should it be the proper study of
all? Were the Ancients mistaken who paid as much
attention to the cultivation of the arts and the study
of moral philosophy? In fact, what is the proper relation
of arts and science in human society? Such questions as
these, though never formulated in so many words, lay
at the back of many men's minds. Sir Thomas Browne,
for example, is recognized today as a pioneer in chemical
embryology. His experiments in that field of science
show, we are told,[1] both originality and genius. Yet in
spite of his scientific ability, Browne had doubts about
the proper study of mankind. Was it not Man, after all,
that Microcosm or little World which contained wonders enough for the most earnest seeker? If it came to a
choice between the two disciplines, Browne had early
decided where his attention must be given:

I could never content my contemplation with
those general pieces of wonder, the Flux and Reflux
of the Sea, the increase of Nile, the conversion of
the Needle to the North; and have studied to
match and parallel those in the more obvious and
neglected pieces of Nature, which without further
travel I can do in the Cosmography of my self. We
carry with us the wonders we seek without us:
there is all Africa and her prodigies in us; we are
that bold and adventurous piece of Nature, which
he that studies wisely learns in a compendium what
others labour at in a divided piece and endless
volume.[2]

That there could be method and discipline in the study
of the mind of Man as much as in the study of the
phenomena of Nature, Locke's *Essay concerning Human
Understanding* was to show. And thus at the end of the
seventeenth century, some men began to express a
revulsion from the too great claims which the scientists
were making. This revulsion of feeling is apparent in

[1] J. Needham *History of Embryology* (1934) 110–12.
[2] *Religio Medici*, I, xv.

certain aspects of the quarrel between the Ancients and the Moderns. Elated by the triumphs of modern scientific discoveries, by the pleasure of correcting venerable and vulgar errors, and more particularly by recognizing that they possessed a new instrument or method of search which promised, in Sir Thomas Browne's words,[1] to complete 'this noble Eluctation of Truth; wherein, against the tenacity of Prejudice and Prescription, this Century now prevaileth', some lay members of the Royal Society, notably Sprat and Glanvill, had congratulated the age a little too heartily on the universal light which illuminated all men's minds, and which contrasted so remarkably with the twilight of ignorance covering ancient Greece and Rome. Such intellectual pride deserved the rebuke which Swift administered in *A Tale of a Tub* and *Gulliver's Travels*, and which Pope was to echo in *The Dunciad*. We are so much accustomed today to treat with respect whatever we hear is going on in a scientist's laboratory, that we have some difficulty in appreciating what is at the back of Swift's satire when Gulliver describes research students at the Academy of Projectors in Laputa calcining ice into gunpowder, experimenting on the softening of marble for pillows and pincushions, and attempting to extract sunbeams from cucumbers, to be put into vials hermetically sealed, and let out to warm the air in raw inclement summers. Yet when we read accounts of the activities of the first Fellows of the Royal Society, we have to admit (while paying honour to those pioneers) that much of what they did was calculated to move the irreverent to incredulous mirth, just because of its apparent triviality. We learn from one account[2] that experiments were made 'of destroying *Mites* by several Fumes: of the equivocal Generation of *Insects*: of feeding a *Carp* in the Air: of making Insects with Cheese, and Sack: of

[1] *Christian Morals*, II, v.
[2] Sprat *History of the Royal Society* (1667) 223.

killing Water-Newts, Toads, and Sloworms with
several Salts: of killing Frogs, by touching their Skin,
with Vinegar, Pitch, or Mercury: of a Spiders not
being inchanted by a Circle of *Vnicorns-horn* . . .
laid round about it'. In such a list as that it is not
difficult for us today to distinguish experiments which
might lead to profitable results, such as the experiment
in disinfestation, from experiments which at best show
mere virtuosity and at the worst are merely fantastic.
But we can surely sympathize with the contemporary
humanist who, lacking the benefit of our perspective
view, dismissed all such stuff with impatience, classify-
ing it with such other Royal Society perversities as
turning 'a piece of roasted mutton into pure blood',[1]
or inquiries from the great Robert Boyle himself about
'the fish that turns to the wind when suspended by a
thread',[2] or demonstrations of artificial serpents 'which
being fired and cast in the water, burnt there to the
bounce.'[3] So that is what these self-satisfied Moderns
mean when they talk about studying God's handi-
work, a humanist might have reflected; experiments
in fireworks and on cheese-mites! Well might Pope's
Goddess of Dullness regard the Fellows of the Royal
Society as her dearest sons, and exhort the rest of
mankind to follow their example:

> O! would the Sons of Men once think their Eyes
> And Reason giv'n them but to study *Flies*!
> See Nature in some partial narrow shape,
> And let the Author of the Whole escape:
> Learn but to trifle; or, who most observe,
> To wonder at their Maker, not to serve.[4]

In those lines Pope pleads, as he had pleaded before, for
a more humanistic conception of study. For him, as for

[1] Pepys *Diary*, 30 May 1667.
[2] C. R. Weld *History of the Royal Society* (1848) i, 107f.
[3] op. cit., i, 116.
[4] *Dunciad*, iv, 453–8.

Pascal,[1] Locke, and Swift, the proper study of mankind is not flies but Man, the Nature of Man, his relations with God and with his fellow-men. This re-emphasis upon the primacy of man, of humane studies, is an attempt to redress the balance which had recently been going in favour of the sciences.

Thus the eighteenth century may be said to have inherited from the seventeenth three closely related problems: how to assimilate the new scientific discoveries, how to reconcile them with traditional beliefs (or how to modify traditional beliefs in the light of what they taught), and how to balance the progress in science with progress in humane studies. These problems are reflected with varying degrees of clarity in the poetry of the eighteenth century; and if these problems are still living problems for us today, as I think they are, then the reflection of them in eighteenth-century poetry merits our attention.

¶ The reconciliation of recent scientific discoveries with traditional beliefs did not appear too difficult. The effect of Sir Isaac Newton's work seemed to confirm that most ancient and cherished belief in an orderly disposed universe, where each created thing had its allowed position and moved in its appointed sphere. The Vast Chain of Being which linked God with the amoeba still held firm, and even Pythagoras's doctrine of attraction seemed to receive fresh force, to be re-expressed in Newton's theory of gravitation.[2] Earlier philosophers had apprehended the divine mechanics of the universe; Newton was felt to have produced demonstrable truth. What had hitherto been darkly apprehended was now clearly seen. Pope, in

[1] J'ai cru trouver au moins bien des compagnons en l'étude de l'homme et que c'est la vraie étude qui lui est propre. J'ai été trompé. Il y en a encore moins qui l'étudient que la géométrie. *Pensées*, ed. Brunschvicg, 144.
[2] A. D. McKillop *The Background of Thomson's Seasons* (1942) 31 ff.

fact, was expressing the view of the educated layman
when he wrote for Newton's epitaph:

> NATURE, and Nature's Laws lay hid in Night.
> God said, *Let Newton be!* and All was *Light*.

And Roger Cotes, the Plumian Professor of Astronomy
at Cambridge, stressed this clarifying effect of Newton's
work in the preface he wrote for the second edition of
the *Principia*, and showed by implication what was
left for the poet to do:

> The gates are now set open, and by his means
> we may freely enter into the knowledge of the
> hidden secrets and wonders of natural things. He
> has so clearly laid open and set before our eyes the
> most beautiful frame of the System of the World,
> that, if King *Alphonsus* were now alive, he would
> not complain for want of the graces either of
> simplicity or of harmony in it. Therefore we may
> now more nearly behold the beauties of Nature,
> and entertain ourselves with the delightful con-
> templation; and, which is the best and most
> valuable fruit of philosophy, be thence incited the
> more profoundly to reverence and adore the
> great MAKER and LORD of all.

That invitation to entertain ourselves with contemplating the beauties of Nature and reverencing the
Creator was written in 1713. And already in the
previous year there had been signs that men of letters
understood the part they were to play. Addison, always
a sensitive witness to the temper of the age, concluded
one of his Saturday speculations in the *Spectator*[1] on the
grounds of faith with a hymn ostensibly versifying the
19th psalm (The Heavens declare the Glory of God),
but betraying in the last verse that men of Newton's
generation, though they could no longer believe in
the music of the spheres, had additional reason for

[1] No. 465.

declaring their faith that the spacious firmament on high was the work of an Almighty hand:

> What though, in solemn Silence, all
> Move round the dark terrestrial Ball?[1]
> What tho' nor real Voice nor Sound
> Amid their radiant Orbs be found?
> *In Reason's Ear* they all rejoice,
> And utter forth a glorious Voice,
> For ever singing, as they shine,
> 'The Hand that made us is Divine'.

Reason's ear was the ear of a generation instructed by Newton, who had given the poets something to sing about, something bold and sublime, as Addison insists. The popularity of nature poetry in the next decade may be attributed, at least in part, to the prestige of Newtonian science, for as Addison remarked:

> Natural Philosophy quickens this Taste of the
> Creation, and renders it not only pleasing to the
> Imagination, but to the Understanding. It does not
> rest in the Murmur of Brooks, and the Melody of
> Birds, in the Shade of Groves and Woods, or in the
> Embroidery of Fields and Meadows, but considers
> the several Ends of Providence which are served
> by them, and the wonders of Divine Wisdom which
> appear in them. It heightens the Pleasures of the
> Eye, and raises such a rational Admiration in the
> Soul as is little inferiour to Devotion.[2]

I do not know whether any but professional students of English Literature regard Thomson's *Seasons* as required reading. Certainly he is no longer what he was for Hazlitt, 'the most popular of all our poets'. But those hundred years of popularity he largely owed to that blend of description and reflection, which Addison prescribed in the words I have just quoted. Thomson's poetry does not rest in the murmur of

---

[1] This line might suggest that Addison was unaffected by post-Copernican astronomy; but see *Spectator*, No. 420.

[2] *Spectator*, No. 393.

brooks and the melody of birds, but considers the wonders of Divine Wisdom which Newton had taught him to see in them. Not for him to wonder idly at the beauty of a rainbow on a spring evening; his rapture is heightened by what Newton had told him:

> Meantime, refracted from yon eastern cloud,
> Bestriding earth, the grand ethereal bow
> Shoots up immense; and every hue unfolds,
> In fair proportion running from the red
> To where the violet fades into the sky.
> Here, awful Newton, the dissolving clouds
> Form, fronting on the sun, thy showery prism;
> And to the sage-instructed eye unfold
> The various twine of light, by thee disclosed
> From the white mingling maze.[1]

His rational admiration is, in Addison's words, little inferior to devotion. When a comet appears, the superstitious and the guilty tremble; but 'the enlightened few,'

> Whose godlike minds philosophy exalts,
> The glorious stranger hail. They feel a joy
> Divinely great;

–they experience, in fact, the authentic thrill of the 'sublime'–

> they in their powers exult,
> That wondrous force of thought, which mounting spurns
> This dusky spot, and measures all the sky.[2]

Thus it comes about that 'tutored' by philosophy, by natural philosophy, that is–a noble term for that noble science we now prefer to call physics–'tutored' by physics,

---

[1] *Spring*, 203–12. Quotations from *The Seasons* are taken from J. Logie Robertson's text (Oxford 1908).
[2] *Summer*, 1714–19.

> hence Poetry exalts
> Her voice to ages; and informs the page
> With music, image, sentiment, and thought,
> Never to die; the treasure of mankind,
> Their highest honour, and their truest joy![1]

The poet, then, so Thomson implies, has a complementary task to that of the natural philosopher—I prefer that term for this purpose to the term 'physicist', which Whewell invented with the term 'scientist' no longer ago than 1840. The natural philosopher's business is to propound a hypothesis which will account satisfactorily for the appearance and behaviour of things. The poet—who should be enough of a scientist to understand what the natural philosopher is doing—presents the synthesis which he sees in the natural philosopher's work, and voices that sense of wonder with which 'the sage-instructed eye' beholds the course of Nature now so satisfactorily explained.

Thomson greets the scientist with words of rapture and tells him what Science has done for at least one poet:

> With thee, serene Philosophy, with thee,
> And thy bright garland, let me crown my song!
> Effusive source of evidence and truth!
> A lustre shedding o'er the ennobled mind,
> Stronger than summer-noon, and pure as that
> Whose mild vibrations soothe the parted soul,
> New to the dawning of celestial day.
> Hence through her nourished powers, enlarged by
>   thee,
> She springs aloft, with elevated pride,
> Above the tangling mass of low desires,
> That bind the fluttering crowd; and, angel-
>   winged,
> The heights of science and of virtue gains,
> Where all is calm and clear.

[1] *Summer*, 1753–7.

There follows a short passage in which Thomson represents the complementary nature of the poet's and the
natural philosopher's tasks:

> with Nature round,
> Or in the starry regions or the abyss,
> To reason's and to fancy's eye displayed –
> The first [*the natural philosopher*] up-tracing, from
>   the dreary void,
> The chain of causes and effects to Him,
> The world-producing Essence, who alone
> Possesses being; while the last [*the poet*] receives
> The whole magnificence of heaven and earth,
> And every beauty, delicate or bold,
> Obvious or more remote, with livelier sense,[1]
> Diffusive painted on the rapid mind.[2]

We should not be surprised that one poet found the
study of physics sublime. What should surprise us is
that there were not more to proclaim the complemen-
tariness of the poet and the physicist, or natural
philosopher, when once it had been announced so
confidently. A few years later Akenside, himself a
scientist, is found acknowledging the inspiration of
Huygens for a passage of astronomical speculation in
The Pleasures of The Imagination;[3] and, like Thomson, he
too confesses that Newton has taught him to contemplate a rainbow with keener delight.[4] But though
neither he nor any other poet of the time shared Thomson's vision of the complementary character of science
and poetry, many agreed with Addison that 'there are
none who more gratifie and enlarge the Imagination,
than the Authors of the new Philosophy, whether we
consider their Theories of the Earth or Heavens, the
Discoveries they have made by Glasses, or any other

---

[1] i.e., with a sensibility keener than the natural philosopher
can claim.

[2] *Summer*, 1730–52.

[3] 5th ed. 1754, i, 201–6.

[4] op. cit., ii, 103–20.

of their Contemplations on Nature'.[1] To the tuition in observation which the scientists had given, we may in part attribute the new enthusiasm for nature description which characterizes eighteenth-century poetry. Despite Dr Johnson's words, poets did 'number the streaks of the tulip', and 'describe the different shades in the verdure of the forest', though usually they were cautious enough to select those features of the individual which every man would regard as typical. Thomson was not the only poet capable of observing that auriculas are 'enriched With shining meal o'er all their velvet leaves'.[2] Crabbe could turn his botanical learning to good effect in describing the stricken land surrounding his Village:

Rank weeds, that every art and care defy,
Reign o'er the land, and rob the blighted rye . . .
There poppies nodding, mock the hope of toil;
There the blue bugloss paints the sterile soil;
Hardy and high, above the slender sheaf,
The slimy mallow waves her silky leaf;
O'er the young shoot the charlock throws a shade,
And clasping tares cling round the sickly blade:[3]

and the contemporaries of Gilbert White had eyes to see 'The chatt'ring Swallow spring'

From the low-roof'd cottage ridge . . .
Darting through the one-arch'd bridge,
    Quick she dips her dappled wing;[4]

or ears to detect how

The scholar bulfinch aims to catch
    The soft flute's iv'ry touch.[5]

In their own medium these less ambitious poets are

[1] *Spectator*, No. 420.
[2] *Spring*, 536f.
[3] *The Village*, I, 67–76.
[4] John Cunningham *Day: A Pastoral* (1763).
[5] Smart *A Song to David* (1763).

responding to the delight in observing natural phenomena which the scientists had awakened. And if
time permitted it would not be difficult to show the
reflection in eighteenth-century poetry of at least
some of the advances in applied science for which the
century is famous. I must be content with pointing out
that Pope found room for Townshend's large-scale
turnip culture in his *Imitations of Horace*,[1] and that Dyer
discovered peculiar material for poetry in the improved
spinning machinery invented by Lewis Paul.[2]

¶ But what of Man in all this? What of the humanist's
fears that Man was forgetting his proper study? Man
was doing very well. Not only was his mind being
studied as it had never been studied before, and his
nature as a social being, but the very poets who found
most to admire in the wonders of Newtonian science
discovered that Man's significance was increased in the
very act of admiration. To no other creature had it
been given to understand the divinely ordered system
of the universe:

> Man superior walks
> Amid the glad creation, musing praise
> And looking lively gratitude.[3]

Thomson and Akenside were convinced that the range
of Man's mental power was sublime. And Pope, a
little grudgingly, agreed. This 'being darkly wise, and
rudely great', as he describes him in the magnificent
opening of the second epistle of *An Essay on Man*, is
'The glory, jest, and riddle of the world'. He proceeds
to elaborate and expound his paradox, and in doing so
he naturally turns to survey the recent triumphs of
scientific method:

[1] *Imitations of Horace*, Ep. II, ii, 273.
[2] *The Fleece*, iii, 292ff.
[3] Thomson *Spring*, 170ff.

> Go, wond'rous creature! mount where Science
>   guides,
> Go, measure earth, weigh air, and state the
>   tides;
> Instruct the planets in what orbs to run,
> Correct old Time, and regulate the Sun . . .
>
> Go, teach Eternal Wisdom how to rule—
> Then drop into thyself, and be a fool!

The descent is, perhaps, a little too boldly abrupt.
What Pope means, as he later explains, is that though
Man has now discovered the rules which bind the
rapid comet, he cannot describe or fix one movement
of his mind:

> Alas what wonder! Man's superior part
> Uncheck'd may rise, and climb from art to art:
> But when his own great work is but begun,
> What Reason weaves, by Passion is undone.

Thus we are brought back to contemplate that conflict which had puzzled the best seventeenth-century
speculations; and with a word or two of advice to the
scientists to take modesty for their guide and eschew
mere virtuosity, mere 'tricks to show the stretch of
human brain', Pope launches into the heart of Man's
proper study, and reveals the strife of Reason and
Passion in the human breast in a series of *Moral Essays*
and *Imitations of Horace*. The metaphysical study of
Man, as exemplified in the *Essay on Man*, has given
place to comedy of manners, a study not of Man's
place in the social scheme but of men's behaviour in
society.

In the process Pope himself approaches near to the
state of Virtuoso, which he so much despised. He does
not, like the objects of his contempt, study flies, or
collect 'Statues, dirty Gods, and Coins',[1] his is a raree-
show of hack journalists, bad poets, booksellers,

[1] *Moral Essays*, IV, 8.

corrupt politicians, pedants, and wealthy city men who did not know how to use their money. All these manners are caught living as they rise and preserved in immortal verse:

> Pretty! in Amber to observe the forms
> Of hairs, or straws, or dirt, or grubs, or worms.

Man, he would have said, is to be studied in living examples, in all the luxurious varieties of eccentricity of which the eighteenth century was so profuse; for in spite of the *Essay on Man*, Pope shared Berkeley's view that Man cannot be studied in the abstract. There was no force in general satire, he felt, and therefore some men had to be pilloried as examples to others. But he was conscious of standards, and was never tired of proclaiming them: the moral character of the good critic is described in the *Essay on Criticism*,[1] and that character represents the standard against which Addison was later to be tried in the character of *Atticus*[2] and found wanting; the wise disposer of his money is discovered in a small Herefordshire town and is set up in the third *Moral Essay*[3] as an example for all to follow; the ideal woman, Candida's great-grandmother (it might be), is described in the second. Do we still recognize her in these lines, I wonder, or has there been a radical change of taste since 1735?

> Oh! blest with Temper, whose unclouded ray
> Can make tomorrow chearful as today;
> She, who can love a Sister's charms, or hear
> Sighs for a Daughter with unwounded ear;
> She, who ne'er answers till a Husband cools,
> Or, if she rules him, never shows she rules;
> Charms by accepting, by submitting sways,
> Yet has her humour most, when she obeys;

[1] 631–42, 729–44.
[2] *Epistle to Dr Arbuthnot*, 193–214.
[3] 249 ff.

Lets Fops or Fortune fly which way they will;
Disdains all loss of Tickets, or Codille;
Spleen, Vapours, or Small-pox, above them all,
And Mistress of herself, tho' China fall.[1]

A change of taste was indeed to be detected within
the next few years. Instead of such a paragon of cheerful self-control as Pope describes, men of the next
generation were to prefer women who, like Fielding's
Sophia Western, loved 'a tender sensation, and would
pay the price of a tear for it at any time',[2] women
whose soft affections, in Henry Mackenzie's phrase,
would 'build their structures, were it but on the paring
of a nail'.[3] These women of sensibility were exactly
matched by the Man of Feeling, a new ideal type who
was beginning to replace the Man of Reason. Even
in Pope's time a man might be expected to mingle the
feast of reason with the flow of soul. In the next
generation, 'strong benevolence of soul' was a first
requirement. The type is early personified in Pope's
young friend, Lyttelton, whose 'tender heart', Thomson tells us,[4] was 'informed by reason's purer ray' and
was the seat of 'animated peace'.

The field of Man which the Man of Feeling beat
was wider than the preserves of the Man of Reason.
Few men can reason to much purpose, but all can *feel*
whatever their education and whatever their rank in
society, though, of course, the more persistently they
cultivated that newly-discovered sixth sense, 'the
moral sense', the more exquisitely their feelings would
respond to all the calls of daily life. Thus we find in the
eighteenth century a gradual widening of the social
conscience; and though we must turn to the novels of
Richardson and Fielding if we would understand how
this new sensibility aroused the social conscience, this

[1] 257–68.
[2] *Tom Jones*, Bk. VI, ch. 5.
[3] *The Man of Feeling*, conclusion.
[4] *Spring*, 904–41.

widening of the social conscience is admirably reflected in the poetry too.

It would be unwise to attribute to the influence of
any one man such a wide-spreading shift in sensibility:
yet if one man is more responsible than another for the
remarkable contemporary spirit of humanitarianism,
that man was Shaftesbury, whose doctrine of 'moral
sense' put a premium on the instinctive responses of
the human heart. It was at any rate in Shaftesbury's
Characteristics that Thomson learned the philosophy of
humanitarianism, which is as recognizable a mark of
his work as his reflection of scientific speculation.
Shaftesbury for him was

> the friend of man,
> Who scanned his nature with a brother's eye,
> His weakness prompt to shade, to raise his aim,
> To touch the finer movements of the mind,
> And with the moral beauty charm the heart.[1]

Taught by Shaftesbury, Thomson invokes his readers'
pity for the poor and the oppressed, for slaves, for the
farm-labourer whose small homestead is overwhelmed
by floods, and utters a 'sigh for suffering worth Lost in
obscurity'.

'Worth lost in obscurity', whether suffering or not,
became a favourite theme in eighteenth-century
poetry. We may remember, perhaps, the still, sad
music of humanity already to be heard before 1720 in
Parnell's *Night Piece on Death*, when the poet meditates on

> Those Graves, with bending Osier bound,
> That nameless heave the crumbled Ground,
> Quick to the glancing Thought disclose
> Where *Toil* and *Poverty* repose.
>
> The flat smooth Stones that bear a Name,
> The Chissels slender help to Fame . . .
> A middle Race of Mortals own,
> Men, half ambitious, all unknown.

[1] *Summer*, 1551-5.

Those lines will insensibly lead our recollections to the more lasting expression which Gray gave to the same theme, when he meditated on the pathos of those mute, inglorious Miltons lying in a country Churchyard:

> Perhaps in this neglected spot is laid
> Some heart once pregnant with celestial fire,
> Hands, that the rod of empire might have sway'd,
> Or wak'd to extasy the living lyre.

> But Knowledge to their eyes her ample page
> Rich with the spoils of time did ne'er unroll;
> Chill Penury repress'd their noble rage,
> And froze the genial current of their soul.

We remember, too, Blake's Little Black Boy and the sad fate of Goldsmith's villagers and of our favourite characters in the poetry of Crabbe. And in this connexion it is worth recalling that Queen Caroline patronized a Wiltshire thresher[1] who had described in halting verse the pitiless rigour of an agricultural labourer's life, that Shenstone could consider a village schoolmistress a fitting subject for a poem of 300 lines, that Dr Johnson wrote his most moving verses on the death of an obscure, uncouth, slum-doctor, a very lowly profession in the eighteenth century, and that (in Carlyle's words) 'A Scottish peasant's life was the meanest and rudest of all lives, till Burns became a poet in it, and a poet of it; found it a *man's* life, and therefore significant to men'[2]. When Burns exclaimed

> What tho' on hamely fare we dine,
>   Wear hodden-gray, and a' that?
> Gie fools their silks, and knaves their wine,
>   A man's a man for a' that,

he was saying more emphatically, as his custom was, what many of his contemporaries had learned to think.

[1] Stephen Duck.
[2] *Edinburgh Review*, December 1828.

¶ Such then were the poetical fruits of mankind's proper study. In pausing at this point, I am stopping too early to gather the full harvest of the years ahead, when a leech-gatherer could be divined as something more than man, when a shepherd on the fells could be seen as

> A solitary object and sublime,
> Above all height! like an aerial Cross,
> Stationed alone upon a spiry Rock
> Of the Chartreuse, for worship,[1]

and when the epitaph of a country girl was to be

> Rolled round in earth's diurnal course,
>   With rocks, and stones, and trees

– in that 'diurnal course' in the heavens which Thomson had contemplated in his sublimest Newtonian moods. Wordsworth's 'passion for the fusion of the human with the impersonal'[2] we have been taught to recognize, and it is in his poetry that we see the fusion of the two disciplines separately reflected in eighteenth-century poetry, the ultimate balancing of the poetry inspired by natural philosophy with the poetry inspired by Man.

1947

[1] Wordsworth *The Prelude*, viii, 272–5.
[2] Basil Willey *The Eighteenth Century Background* (1940) 288.

7

Pope and the Opposition to Walpole's Government

Pope's excursion into politics did not last long. His political poems cover no more than the years 1733 to 1740, and even during those years there were periods when his interest was deflected to other affairs. Yet short as the excursion was, it deserves some attention from historians, since Pope expressed in memorable verse the moral objections felt towards Walpole's government. Furthermore, Pope was the exception amongst contemporary men of letters in that he had nothing to gain personally from either party in the state. He was a Roman Catholic at a time when Catholics were still liable to persecution. He could hold no office, and he derived no income from party funds. And so his attack on the Government was, if not absolutely disinterested, at any rate the nearest thing we are likely to find to an attack based purely on moral principles.

First, let me remind you of what was happening at that time in parliament and in its lobbies. Walpole had been in power since 1721, except for one brief interval immediately after George II's accession to the throne. His position was secure, partly because Queen Caroline—and therefore George II—had confidence in him, partly because he and the Duke of Newcastle knew how to manage the elections, and partly because he met with no effectual opposition in Parliament. The

Tories had been out of countenance since Queen Anne's death, retained a mere shadow of their former power, and were divided in aim. One group, led by Shippen, was openly Jacobite in sympathy, the other, led by a convert from Jacobitism, Sir William Wyndham, had accepted the new dynasty and were known as the Hanover Tories. The number of Walpole's opponents was also increased from time to time by discontented Whigs, such as Carteret and the two Pulteneys, men of considerable intellectual ability—indeed, of too great intellectual ability to live happily with Walpole, who preferred a good 'yes'-man like Sir William Yonge or Winnington for a colleague. But the growth of the opposition in numbers merely served to emphasize its factiousness. Walpole's opponents could not formulate any alternative policy, because they were too deeply divided and therefore their attack was either conventional—the hoary old policy of attacking the Government for maintaining a large standing army in time of peace—or merely opportunist. Such an opportunity had arisen in 1733 when Walpole contemplated a warehousing scheme designed to make London a free port and England a storehouse for the temporary deposit of goods. The Opposition seized this opportunity and misinterpreted Walpole's intention so as to make his measure look like a general excise, 'a hateful tax', to quote Johnson's *Dictionary*, 'levied upon commodities, and adjudged not by the common judges of property, but wretches hired by those to whom excise is paid'. The outcry both inside and outside parliament was so loud that Walpole withdrew his bill. The prospects of the Opposition had never looked brighter, for Walpole's prestige at Court was lowered by this defeat, and a general election was close at hand. But when the election came twelve months later, it was already too late; for the essential factiousness of the Opposition had once more been demonstrated in the apathetic support given by Pulteney to the Tories' attempted repeal of the Septennial Act.

Walpole regained his ascendency over the new Parliament and held it for another three uneventful years, in spite of the Opposition being strengthened by a new group, a group of young Whigs: Lyttelton, Polwarth (later Lord Marchmont), Murray (later Lord Mansfield), and a formidable young Cornet of Horse elected for the first time, whose name was William Pitt. This group was contemptuously referred to by Government supporters as the Boy Patriots, or more shortly, as the Boys; and it is with the Boys that we shall find Pope intimately associated.

Walpole's difficulties began to increase in 1737. An Opposition bill for enlarging the Prince of Wales's allowance was defeated by a narrow Government majority in both houses. In April Parliament discussed what punishment should be inflicted upon the city of Edinburgh for the Porteous riots, and Walpole was forced to whittle down the bill of penalties as a result of strong opposition from the Duke of Argyle. In November, his most faithful supporter, Queen Caroline, died. At the same time Walpole's policy of avoiding foreign entanglements was being endangered by the recurrent raids of Spanish ships on English merchantmen; and (as every schoolboy knows), in March 1738, Captain Jenkins exhibited to a sympathetic committee of the House of Commons an ear of which he had been deprived by a Spanish captain nearly eight years before. Walpole was losing control of the situation, yet the Parliamentary Opposition still remained dissident and ineffectual, because its leaders were still unable to agree upon a concerted policy of attack.

Such was the political situation inside Parliament. Outside Parliament Walpole had at least two important enemies to reckon with. One was Frederick, Prince of Wales, who (like every other Hanoverian heir) was at loggerheads with his father, and consequently with his father's chief minister. Some attempt has recently been made to rehabilitate 'poor Fred'; it is sufficient for my present purpose to recall that certain sections of the Parliamentary Opposition looked to him for encouragement and even leadership, and that so far as Frederick was capable of encouraging and leading, encourage he did and lead he did whenever he saw an opportunity of inconveniencing his father and mother.

Walpole's other enemy of note was Bolingbroke, who had returned from exile in 1723, pardoned for complicity with the Jacobites, but forbidden to resume his seat in the House of Lords. Bolingbroke knew that he could never regain power except by Walpole's defeat; but, as he was excluded from Parliament, his only means of attack was to conduct a press campaign and to direct such members of the Opposition as would trust him. In the pages of *The Craftsman* he did what he could to unite the dissident elements of the Opposition. There is no doubt that he chose the right tactical approach. The time was past, he declared, when differences existed between Whigs and Tories, for honest men of both parties accepted the principles of the Revolution as a statement of political orthodoxy. They must therefore unite against the common enemy, who is fostering corruption, endeavouring to make a standing army in time of peace a part of the constitution, and concealing frauds and protecting the fraudulent at the risk of ruining credit and destroying trade. I have called this good tactics, but it was more than that. It was an astute diagnosis of the political position, for party labels had begun to lose their meaning under the early Hanoverians. The Tories were no longer the Church Party at a time when most of the bishops supported Walpole, nor was there any longer a clear division of parties on the issue of the Succession. The division now was between the Court Party, the party in Power, and the Country Party; and there is little doubt that Walpole owed much of his parliamentary success to the fact that he himself was a country squire who could talk to other squires of the opposing party in a language they understood.

If we measure Bolingbroke's statement of policy by its political results, we might not rate its appeal very high. But there was at least one man to whom it appealed most strongly, and that man was Bolingbroke's neighbour and intimate friend, Alexander Pope. Some sort of case can be made for the view that Pope's philosophical and political theories were entirely derived from Bolingbroke, and indeed many parallels can be found between the political doctrines of *The Craftsman* and Pope's *Imitations of Horace*; but I think it would be truer to say that Pope and Bolingbroke reached the same conclusion from different premises. Pope had never been a party man. In Queen Anne's reign, when Whig and Tory still implied some fundamental difference, Pope had friends in both parties and showed not the least enthusiasm for their political differences. Although he has left us in one poem, *The Rape of the Lock*, and in that poem only, a brilliant reflection of society at the Court of Queen Anne, he was constitutionally unfitted either for society life or for coffee-house life. He tried both for a very short time about the year 1712, but he soon abandoned them and spent the rest of his days in the country houses of his friends and in his own country houses, first at Chiswick and later at Twickenham. I will not say he was a countryman; and when I remember Wordsworth I cannot call him a country poet; but there have been few poets since Horace so devoted to the ideal of contentment with a modest competence, an ideal most easily realized, so Horace thought, in country surroundings. This sober Epicureanism is the mainspring of Pope's moral poetry from the year 1733 onwards when he began to publish a series of essays in verse entitled the *Ethic Epistles*. The work was never completed, but we possess what was to have been the first book, entitled *An Essay on Man*, in four epistles, as well

as four more essays on the *Characters of Men and Women*
and on the *Use of Riches*, a group usually known as the
Moral Essays. It is these poems, together with a series
called the *Imitations of Horace*, also started in 1733, with
which I shall concern myself.

Pope was not a systematic thinker. The scraps of
Platonism, Deism, Optimism, Positivism, and Epicureanism, which he tried to piece together into a system,
provokes contemptuous mirth from the professional
philosophers. But even the philosophers allow the value
of his moral intuitions, while they mock his attempts
to systematize them. Of these intuitions, the most important is the cult of non-attachment. Try to cultivate
a serenity of mind, Pope says, which will make you
impervious to the buffets of fortune. Don't found your
happiness on your intellectual parts, on what your rank
in society brings, on the beneficence of your administration as a statesman; don't rely for happiness on the
prospect of fame; above all, don't rely on money. Yet
if you have money, learn this at least, to use it wisely.

We have heard this sort of thing plenty of times, and
so had Pope's readers in the eighteenth century. But it
was characteristic of those days that no man resented
being told the same thing time and time again so long
as it was true and so long as it was said with fresh
conviction. Indeed the older and the more familiar the
doctrine the better, for if a doctrine had been tested by
one generation after another that successive testing
seemed to assure its universal validity. Addison,
reviewing Pope's *Essay on Criticism* in the *Spectator*, puts
this point very well:

> Give me leave to mention what Monsieur *Boileau*
> has so very well enlarged upon in the Preface to
> his Works, that Wit and fine Writing doth not con-
> sist so much in advancing things that are new, as
> in giving things that are known an agreeable Turn.
> It is impossible, for us who live in the later Ages of
> the World, to make Observations in Criticism,

> Morality, or in any Art or Science, which have not
> been touched upon by others. We have little else
> left us, but to represent the common Sense of
> Mankind in more strong, more beautiful, or more
> uncommon Lights.[1]

How then did Pope represent the common sense of
mankind in uncommon lights? The answer is that he
did not content himself with maxims, though his
maxims have passed into the proverbial heritage of the
language. He illustrates: he shows what he means by
non-attachment or by contentment with a modest
competence, and he draws his illustrations from his own
life or from the lives of his friends.

> Content with little, I can piddle here
> On Broccoli and mutton, round the year;
> But ancient friends, (tho' poor, or out of play)
> That touch my Bell, I cannot turn away.
> 'Tis true, no Turbots dignify my boards,
> But gudgeons, flounders, what my Thames affords.[2]

It is characteristic of Pope, that he rarely sees the
good without also seeing the bad in conflict with it.
The strong antipathy of good to bad was, as he explains on one occasion, the very provocation of his
satire. And so it pleased him to represent two con-
flicting sets of values: the old Roman simplicity of that
secluded villa at Twickenham on the one hand, on the
other the luxury and deceitfulness of life at Court and
in the City; or (in more individual terms) the philan-
thropy of a Ralph Allen on the one hand, who 'did
good by stealth and blush'd to find it fame', and on the
other the colossal frauds perpetrated on the widows
and the poor by Blunt of the South Sea Company and
Bond of the Charitable Corporation.

To a modern reader such a contrast is purely moral.
To a reader of the 1730s the contrast was only partly

[1] *Spectator*, 253.
[2] *Imitations of Horace*, Sat. II, ii, 137–42.

moral: the political relevance was equally clear, for (as I have said) the party division was less a division between Whig and Tory, than a division between Court and Country; and Pope was serving the interests of the Opposition by representing with all his power the contrast of moral values underlying the political conflict.

There is no poem which represents this moral yet political contrast so clearly as the *Imitation of the First Epistle of the First Book of Horace*, addressed to Bolingbroke. I choose a central passage, where one is able to detect not merely the contrast between the two sets of moral values, but political contrast, evident in the innuendo at the expense of Walpole and the Court.

> Yet every child another song will sing,
> 'Virtue, brave boys! 'tis Virtue makes a King.'
> True, conscious Honour is to feel no sin,
> He's arm'd without that's innocent within;
> Be this thy Screen, and this thy Wall of Brass;
> Compar'd to this, a Minister's an Ass.
>
> And say, to which shall our applause belong,
> This new Court jargon, or the good old song?
> The modern language of corrupted Peers,
> Or what was spoke at CRESSY and POITIERS?
>
> Who counsels best? who whispers, 'Be but Great,
> With Praise or Infamy, leave that to fate;
> Get Place and Wealth, if possible, with Grace;
> If not, by any means get Wealth and Place.'[1]

One can see what is at the bottom of Pope's objection. It is the improper regard for money. He sees this alike in the city, where these new Whig financiers gain control of trusts and charitable corporations, in the army, at court, and in parliament, where, as Walpole himself declared, 'all these men have their price'.[2]

[1] 91–104.
[2] I like to think that Pope was glancing at this wide-spread political subservience to the man who paid best, when he wrote an epigram for the collar of the Prince of Wales's dog – at any

And what can be done about it? Pope's answer to that question was twofold. He could use his satire to expose vicious behaviour:

> Brand the bold Front of shameless, guilty Men,
> Dash the proud Gamester in his gilded Car,
> Bare the mean Heart that lurks beneath a Star[1]

and, secondly, he could hold up for imitation some better standard. The exposure of vice raised the question of the ethics of personal satire. Was he justified in singling one or two individuals from the crowd? Would it not be more charitable to deal with the vicious in gross? He had no doubt about the correct course to take: 'General Satire in Times of General Vice', he told his friend, Arbuthnot, 'has no force and is no Punishment: People have ceas'd to be ashamed of it when so many are joind with them; and 'tis only by hunting One or two from the Herd that any Examples can be made.'[2] It is a theme to which he loves to return. He discusses it for the last time in *The Epilogue to the Satires*; notice how he infers that all virtue rests with the Opposition, with individuals who in one way or another have quarrelled with Walpole:

> But does the Court a worthy Man remove?
> That instant, I declare, he has my Love:
> I shun his Zenith, court his mild Decline:
> Thus SOMMERS once, and HALIFAX were mine.
> Oft in the clear, still Mirrour of Retreat,
> I study'd SHREWSBURY, the wise and great:
> CARLETON's calm Sense, and STANHOPE's
>   noble Flame,
> Compar'd, and knew their gen'rous End the same:
> How pleasing ATTERBURY's softer hour!

---

rate, it epitomizes a good deal of the parliamentary situation: 'I am His Highness' Dog at *Kew*; Pray tell me Sir, whose Dog are you?'.

[1] *Imitations of Horace*, Sat. II, i, 106–8.
[2] 2 August, 1734.

How shin'd the Soul, unconquer'd in the Tow'r!
How can I PULT'NEY, CHESTERFIELD forget,
While *Roman* Spirit charms, and *Attic* Wit:
ARGYLE, the State's whole Thunder born to
    wield,
And shake alike the Senate and the Field:
Or WYNDHAM, just to Freedom and the Throne,
The Master of our Passions, and his own.
Names, which I long have lov'd, nor lov'd in vain,
Rank'd with their Friends, not number'd with their
    Train;
And if yet higher the proud List should end,
Still let me say! No Follower, but a Friend.[1]

'If yet higher the proud List should end' is clearly a reference to the Prince of Wales, who is thus put in what Pope considers his right place as a leader of all those virtuous men who oppose Walpole.

Proceeding, then, to his attack, Pope singles out one or two notorious public figures who represent luxury and corruption in various manifestations. There is Denis Bond, expelled from the House of Commons in 1732 for breach of trust and found guilty of embezzling the funds of the Charitable Corporation shortly after, yet so little discredited that in 1735 we find him appointed a churchwarden of St George's, Hanover Square. There is Francis Chartres, a most notorious debauchee, who amassed a fortune by gambling and usury. There is Gilbert Heathcote, the Governor of the Bank of England and the richest commoner in the country, who was nevertheless so mean as to dispute the cost of his brother's funeral fees with the parson of his parish; and there is John Ward, MP for Weymouth, convicted of fraud and forgery, who amused himself during his term of imprisonment by giving poison to dogs and cats, to see them expire by slower or quicker torments. I could extend Pope's list by mentioning

[1] *Epilogue to the Satires*, Dia. II, 74–93.

minor court officials and small office-holders as well as pseudonymous characters of uncertain identity, such as Timon, the tasteless Magnifico, and Sir Balaam, the City Knight, who came to a bad end through speculation and accepting bribes from the French; but my list is representative. None of these figures is an eminent politician, though the political allegiance of every one of them was Whig. It would not have suited Pope's purpose to single out men who were known merely for their political allegiance. What he wishes to emphasize is that it is such men as these who prosper under Walpole's administration, and that the administration is favourable to the spread of corruption in all walks of life. Walpole himself comes off lightly; for Pope, who loved his own Twickenham retreat, was not without sympathy for the man who preferred the shades of Houghton to the well-dressed rabble of St James's. But even his compliments to Walpole on his non-attachment are tainted with innuendo:

> Go see Sir ROBERT – See Sir ROBERT!–hum–
> And never laugh–for all my life to come?
> Seen him I have, but in his happier hour
> Of Social Pleasure, ill-exchang'd for Pow'r;
> Seen him, uncumber'd with the Venal tribe,
> Smile without Art, and win without a Bribe.
> Would he oblige me? let me only find,
> He does not think me what he thinks mankind.
> Come, come, at all I laugh He laughs, no doubt,
> The only diff'rence is, I dare laugh out.[1]

Such a left-handed compliment weighs very light against such an obvious reference as this to the effect of Walpole's policy:

> Much injur'd Blunt! why bears he Britain's hate?
> A wizard told him in these words our fate:
> 'At length Corruption, like a gen'ral flood,

---

[1] *Epilogue to the Satires*, Dia. I, 27–36.

> (So long by watchful Ministers withstood)
> Shall deluge all; and Av'rice creeping on,
> Spread like a low-born mist, and blot the Sun;
> Statesman and Patriot ply alike the stocks,
> Peeress and Butler share alike the Box,
> And Judges job, and Bishops bite the town,
> And mighty Dukes pack cards for half a crown.
> See Britain sunk in lucre's sordid charms,
> And France reveng'd of ANNE's and EDWARD's
>   arms!'[1]

But the picture is not wholly black. The very fact of contrast, of that strong antipathy of good to bad, suggests that in Sodom and Gomorrah there are still some righteous men left; and they are to be found (of course) amongst the ranks of the Parliamentary Opposition. In his brief characters of these men, Pope builds up his standard of political and moral probity. Have we been sickened by ministerial equivocation? Very well, let us observe the leader of the Jacobite Tories:

> I love to pour out all myself, as plain
> As downright *Shippen*, or as old *Montagne*.[2]

Have we been disgusted by these pictures of meanness and depravity? Very well:

> Would ye be blest? despite low Joys, low Gains:
> Disdain whatever CORNBURY disdains;
> Be Virtuous, and be happy for your pains.[3]

Does the spirit of patriotism seem dead? Then we need only look at another of the 'Boys' in the new Parliament:

> Sometimes a Patriot, active in debate,
> Mix with the World, and battle for the State,

[1] *Moral Essays*, III, 135–46.
[2] *Imitations of Horace*, Sat. II, i, 51–2.
[3] op. cit., Ep. I, vi, 60–2.

> Free as young Lyttelton, her cause pursue,
> Still true to Virtue, and as warm as true:[1]

– or at one of the older Whigs dismissed from office by Walpole:

> And you! brave C O B H A M, to the latest breath
> Shall feel your ruling passion strong in death:
> Such in those moments as in all the past,
> 'Oh, save my country, Heav'n!' shall be your last.[2]

Is there no example of non-attachment in this world of greedy and grasping politicians? Certainly there is, and Pope is not afraid to proclaim him even though the Government has declared that Harley is a public enemy (I quote from a poem written ten years earlier):

> And sure if ought below the Seats Divine
> Can touch Immortals, 'tis a Soul like thine:
> A Soul supreme, in each hard Instance try'd,
> Above all Pain, all Passion, and all Pride,
> The Rage of Pow'r, the Blast of publick Breath,
> The Lust of Lucre, and the Dread of Death.[3]

It is not without reason that Hazlitt declared: 'Pope's compliments are divine'. You will say, perhaps, that Pope's is an oblique method of political attack, and you may well doubt whether such a method could succeed. The Government felt the force of it, however. After the publication in 1738 of the two dialogues called *An Epilogue to the Satires*, the Government replied, equally obliquely, by summoning Pope's friend, Whitehead, before the House of Lords to answer for a libellous satire, called *Manners*. The action was recognized on all sides as a plain warning to Pope. Pope took the warning, and when preparing the *Epilogue* for reissue in 1744 he added this note to the last line:

> This was the last poem of the kind printed by our author, with a resolution to publish no more; but

[1] op. cit., Ep. I, i, 27–30.   [2] *Moral Essays* I, 262–5.
[3] *Epistle to Robert Earl of Oxford*, 21–6.

> to enter thus, in the most plain and solemn
> manner he could, a sort of P R O T E S T against that
> insuperable corruption and depravity of manners,
> which he had been so unhappy as to live to see.
> Could he have hoped to have amended any, he had
> continued those attacks; but bad men were grown
> so shameless and so powerful, that Ridicule was
> become as unsafe as it was ineffectual.

That was his last word in public. But there survives a strange fragment called *1740*, evidently written to describe the political scene in that year, but never completed and not published until fifty years later. His hopes from the Parliamentary Opposition, like the hopes of Bolingbroke, were dead after Wyndham died in that year. Listen to his review of the possibilities:

> Carteret, his own proud dupe, thinks Monarchs
>   things
> Made just for him, as other fools for Kings;
> Controls, decides, insults thee every hour,
> And antedates the hatred due to Pow'r.

As for Pulteney, he (it seemed) had been silenced by the promise of a peerage:

> Thro' Clouds of Passion Pulteney's views are
>   clear,
> He foams a Patriot to subside a Peer;
> Impatient sees his country bought and sold,
> And damns the market where he takes no gold.[1]

If we were to rely on the Jacobite, Shippen, for a remedy, we should be let in for a bloody revolution:

> To purge and let thee blood, with fire and sword,
> Is all the help stern Shippen wou'd afford.

Even the Boys have proved disappointing:

> That those who bind and rob thee, would not kill,
> Good Cornbury hopes, and candidly sits still.[2]

[1] *One Thousand Seven Hundred and Forty*, 5–12.
[2] op. cit., 15–18.

And as for the rest, the Tory country squires

> . . . each winter up they run,
> And all are clear, that something must be done.
> Then urg'd by Carteret, or by Carteret stopt,
> Inflam'd by Pulteney, or by Pulteney dropt;
> They follow rev'rently each wond'rous wight,
> Amaz'd that one can read, that one can write:
> So geese to gander prone obedience keep,
> Hiss if he hiss, and if he slumber, sleep.
> Till having done whate'er was fit or fine,
> Utter'd a speech, and ask'd their friends to dine;
> Each hurries back to his paternal ground,
> Contend but for five shillings in the pound,
> Yearly defeated, yearly hopes they give,
> And all agree, Sir Robert cannot live.[1]

Then wherein lies our hope? Pope knew Frederick, Prince of Wales, and had been admitted to a private view of Bolingbroke's *Idea of a Patriot King* in manuscript. A letter to Lyttelton, the Prince's secretary, written in November 1738, shows the way Pope's mind was working: 'Pray assure your Master', he writes, 'of my Duty and Service: They tell me he has everybody's Love already. I wish him Popular, but not Familiar, and the Glory of being beloved, not the Vanity of endeavouring it too much. I wish him at the Head of the Only Good Party in the Kingdom, that of Honest Men.'[2] And in the poem *1740*, Pope enlarged this into a statement of practical politics: it is the policy of the Patriot King:

> Alas! on one alone our all relies,
> Let him be honest, and he must be wise,
> Let him no trifler from his   school,
> Nor like his . . . still a . . .
> Be but a man! unministered, alone,
> And free at once the Senate and the Throne;

[1] op. cit., 29–42.
[2] *Correspondence*, ed. G. Sherburn (Oxford 1956) IV, 143–4.

> Esteem the public love his best supply,
> A King's true glory his integrity;
> Rich *with* his Britain, *in* his Britain strong,
> Affect no conquest, but endure no wrong.
> Whatever his religion or his blood,
> His public virtue makes his title good.
> Europe's just balance and our own may stand,
> And one man's honesty redeem the land.[1]

Throughout the last year or two of his life Pope ceased to take an active interest in politics, contenting himself (as he told his friend, Ralph Allen) 'with honest wishes, for honest men to govern us, without asking for any Party, or Denomination, beside'.[2] But he had done his work: he had aroused the public conscience, which was to be kept awake in the next generation by the writings of such men as the Reverend John Brown, a former Rector of this City[3]; he had made a notable contribution towards 'renewing a right spirit within us'.

1946

[1] *1740*, 85–98.
[2] *Correspondence*, IV, 387, 8 February 1741/2.
[3] Rector of St Nicholas, Newcastle upon Tyne, 1761–6.
Author of *An Estimate of the Manners and Principles of the Times*, 1757.

8

Dickens's Christmas Books

I propose to limit myself to the five short books which Dickens published between 1843 and 1848, namely *A Christmas Carol*, *The Chimes*, *The Cricket on the Hearth*, *The Battle of Life*, and *The Haunted Man*. The first of these has indeed retained most of its great contemporary popularity; but who now reads *The Chimes* and *The Cricket*? Very few, I suspect; and fewer still recall even the names of *The Battle of Life* and *The Haunted Man*. My subject then is avowedly minor Dickens, but I shall submit that it is none the less interesting. And the interest to my mind lies chiefly in this, that the Christmas Books mark an important stage in Dickens's development as a novelist.

Let me begin by setting them in their historical place in Dickens's career. In 1843, when the *Carol* was published, Dickens was aged thirty-one. He was still a young man, that is to say; but he was already a household name both in England and in America. This popularity had been suddenly gained six years earlier during the publication of *Pickwick Papers* in monthly numbers, and each succeeding novel had added to that popularity: *Oliver Twist* in 1837-8, *Nicholas Nickleby* in 1838-9, and *The Old Curiosity Shop* in 1840. He had shown in those early books that he knew how to move his readers both to laughter and to tears; he had drawn a wide diversity of scenes, in town and country, in London and the provinces, though he appeared on the whole to move more easily amongst the poor and the lower middle classes than amongst their social superiors. He had shown abundantly that he possessed an eye for significant detail and an ear to detect those distinguishing qualities of speech that can mark a man off from his fellows. Above all, he seemed able to draw on an inexhaustible spring of human sympathy, of sympathy not merely for human distress but also for every manifestation of human brotherhood. And with this sympathy went a strong distaste for institutionalism, and for persons who preferred to perform their social duties through the medium of an institution, whether it be a Board of Guardians or the House of Commons, instead of taking individual action to relieve individual distress.

Furthermore the strength of his appeal to his reader's emotions was reinforced by traditional means. A reader bred up on the eighteenth-century novel must have recognized immediately where he stood. There was nothing unfamiliar in the manner of the appeal to set up that resistance which the mass of readers always present to what they are unaccustomed to. Here they found the characters of Smollett come to life once more. Here were Smollett's rogues and Smollett's eccentrics acting in the sort of slum conditions in which Smollett had set them; but the showmanship with which they were displayed recalled rather the showmanship of Sterne. It is true that Boz never cut the absurd capers of Shandy. But he had evidently learned from Shandy how to buttonhole his reader, how to confide in him as man to man, and to laugh or to weep in his presence with complete absence of reserve. This combination proved irresistible. We might expect that the defences of the unsophisticated reader would soon be down; but even the more experienced critics of the older generation gave in one by one. Leigh Hunt exclaimed that Fanny Squeers's letter to Ralph

Nickleby surpassed the best things of the kind in Smollett. Sydney Smith succumbed to the charms of Mrs Nickleby: 'I stood out against Mr Dickens as long as I could', he wrote, after the sixth monthly number, 'but he has conquered me'. Jeffrey, his fellow-writer in the *Edinburgh Review*, was vanquished by Little Nell: there had been nothing so good, he was accustomed to say, 'since Cordelia'; while Landor ranked her with Juliet and Desdemona.[1]

It is astonishing to reflect that all this was achieved in less than five years. But the achievement was costly. Forster tells us that as early as 1839, after completing *Nicholas Nickleby*, Dickens was beginning to feel the strain upon his powers of invention. It was in that year that he put forward a proposal for relieving himself of this strain by launching a new periodical under his own general direction but of which he would not himself be the sole author. The periodical was to begin, like the *Spectator*, with 'a little club or knot of characters' whose personal histories and proceedings would be carried through the work; amusing essays would be written on 'the various foibles of the day as they arise'; and the form of the papers would be varied 'by throwing them into sketches, essays, tales, adventures, letters from imaginary correspondents and so forth'. There would also be a series of papers 'containing stories and descriptions of London as it was many years ago, as it is now, and as it will be many years hence, to which', writes Dickens, 'I would give some such title as The Relaxations of Gog and Magog, dividing them into portions like the *Arabian Nights*, and supposing Gog and Magog to entertain each other with such narrations in the Guildhall all night long, and to break off every morning at daylight'. Lastly there would be 'a series of satirical papers purporting to be translated from some Savage Chronicles, and to describe the administration of justice in some country that never

[1] Forster *Life of Dickens*, II, iv, vii, x.

existed', whose object would be 'to keep a special look-out upon the magistrates in town and country, and never to leave those worthies alone'.[1]

This highly characteristic scheme shows that Dickens had not yet fully outgrown those *Sketches* with which his career as a writer had begun a mere three years earlier, and which had been published in the daily and weekly press. He was still a journalist at heart – it might be argued that he never entirely ceased to be a journalist – and for guidance in formulating his fancies he reverted to the practices of eighteenth-century journalism, as Addison, Swift, and Goldsmith understood it.

We may doubt whether this plan would have served the purpose he had in view. He intended to enlist the help of a team of subordinates in putting it into practice; but he would surely still have been taxing his powers of invention by incessant improvisation. The looseness of the form proposed would have done nothing to control or direct his imagination. In the event he abandoned the scheme during the course of the first month, and for the remainder of its existence this new periodical, *Master Humphrey's Clock*, was to be no more than the means of publishing that extraordinary improvisation *The Old Curiosity Shop*, and of completing the abandoned novel *Barnaby Rudge*.

Thus two more years had passed, and Dickens was no nearer to solving the problem of conserving his inventive powers. He could restock his mind, however, and this he did by visiting America after bringing *Barnaby Rudge* to a conclusion. But though America could supply him with new material, not merely for one book, but for a considerable portion of a second, it could not provide the solution to his problem. How was he to relieve the strain upon his inventive faculty?

¶ We have now come to 1843, the year of *A Christmas*
    [1] *Life*, II, vi.

Carol. Throughout the year Dickens had been engaged in writing and publishing *Martin Chuzzlewit.* This novel might be claimed as the last of his first period, the last to be undertaken haphazardly, with little view at the outset (to quote the words of Forster, his biographer) of 'the main track of his design'. And it was the last which could possibly have admitted such a desperate improvisation as that of sending the young hero and his squire to America. But though it is so defective in its story and structure, there are some signs of a new beginning, and of a beginning which might serve to discipline his powers. Dickens tells us himself in the preface (1844) that he has 'endeavoured . . . to resist the temptation of the current Monthly Number, and to keep a steadier eye upon the general purpose and design' of the tale; and Forster informs us that the difficulties he encountered were 'such as to render him, in his subsequent stories, more bent upon constructive care at the outset'.[1] The design, says Forster, was 'to show, more or less by every person introduced, the number and variety of humours and vices that have their root in selfishness'; but what was still lacking was a plot to carry or embody that design. When we turn to the next twenty-month serial novel, *Dombey and Son*, published in 1846–8 – three years later, that is to say – we already find that a suitable plot to carry the design has been discovered, and from the time of *Dombey and Son* onwards there is no backsliding, unless it be in *David Copperfield*; while before him lie such masterpieces of constructive power as *Bleak House*, *A Tale of Two Cities*, and *Great Expectations*. The years intervening between *Martin Chuzzlewit* and *Dombey and Son* would seem therefore to be crucial for his development as a novelist; and these are the years of the Christmas Books.

The fancy of writing a Christmas book occurred to Dickens when he was at Manchester in the first week

[1] *Life*, IV, i.

of October 1843. On his return in the second week he
set to work on *A Christmas Carol* and completed it by
the end of November. We know something about the
drift of his thoughts during these weeks, for he was
much occupied in advising Miss Coutts on how best to
distribute her charities, which seem to have been
specially directed at that time towards the care of
destitute children. He had paid a visit to a Ragged
School on her behalf in mid-September, and had sent
her what he called 'a sledge-hammer account' of the
place.[1] At the same time he had written to the editor
of the *Edinburgh Review*, laying stress on the state of
ignorance, misery, and neglect which he found there.[2]

His visit to Manchester was also on charitable
business. He was to preside at the first annual Soirée
of the Athenaeum, a sort of working man's institute,
and he took the occasion for speaking about the
education of the poor. This institution, he said, offered
'blameless rational enjoyment . . . to every youth
and man in this great town'. And the effect would be
that though a man 'should find it hard for a season even
to keep the wolf of hunger from his door, let him but
once have chased the dragon of ignorance from his
hearth, and self-respect and hope are left him'. Nor
need the Manchester employer fear what a little
learning may do, for 'the more a man who improves
his leisure in such a place learns, the better, gentler,
kinder man he must become. When he knows how
much great minds have suffered for the truth in every
age and time, and to what dismal persecutions opinion

[1] 16 September 1843; printed in *Letters from Charles Dickens
to Angela Burdett Coutts*, ed. Edgar Johnson (London 1953) 50–4.
In March he had been 'so perfectly stricken down' by a blue book
sent to him by Southwood Smith that he contemplated writing
'a very cheap pamphlet called An Appeal to the People of England
on behalf of the Poor Man's Child'. This was abandoned a few
days later in favour of a 'sledge-hammer' blow (*Letters*, ed.
W. Dexter, 1938, I, 512). He may already have foreseen an
appeal something like *A Christmas Carol*.
[2] *Letters*, I, 540.

has been exposed, he will become more tolerant of other men's belief in all matters, and will incline more leniently to their sentiments when they chance to differ from his own. Understanding that the relations between himself and his employers involve a mutual duty and responsibility, he will discharge his part of the implied contract cheerfully, faithfully, and honourably; for the history of every useful life warns him to shape his course in that direction'.[1]

The care of poor children, the banishment of ignorance as one means of banishing poverty, the establishment of relations of 'mutual duty and responsibility' between employer and employed: while his mind was running on these subjects, Dickens had also to apply himself to the next number of the novel on which he was at work. This novel was *Martin Chuzzlewit*. No. x (chapters xxiv–xxvi), in which the marriage of Mercy Pecksniff to Jonas Chuzzlewit is related, had been published a few days before he set out for Manchester. The chapters, therefore, which he was writing concurrently with the *Carol* are those chapters in no. xi (chapters xxvii–xxix) describing a swindle named the Anglo-Bengalee Disinterested Loan and Life Assurance Company, and the rapacity and humbug of its three promoters, Montague Tigg, David Crimple, and Mr Jobling. And before the Number is brought to an end we are allowed a glance at humbug and self-seeking in other walks of life, in the shape of Mrs Gamp, so full of zeal for her patients that she 'worrits' herself, and of Mr Mould, the undertaker, civilly greeting an invalid with a view to his future custom.[2]

Thus, Dickens's thoughts in October 1843 were running upon humbug, self-seeking, and rapacity, as well as upon the care of poor children, the banishment of ignorance, and the duties and responsibilities of

[1] *Speeches of Charles Dickens*, ed. K. J. Fielding (Oxford 1960) 46–9.
[2] Chapter xxix.

employer and employed. But what also is more likely
than that, when meditating his first Christmas book,
he should return in mind to the last story he had
written for Christmas? The ninth monthly number of
Pickwick Papers (chapters xxviii–xxx) was published in
December 1836, and was clearly intended to suit the
Christmas season. In that number Mr Pickwick and his
friends go down to Dingley Dell to celebrate Christmas
with Mr Wardle and his family. The principal cere-
monies at Dingley Dell are feasting and dancing with
the whole household, servants and all, collected together, and the time is whiled away on Christmas Eve
with songs, forfeits, and old stories. One of these old
stories has a chapter to itself,[1] and it is important for
our purpose. It is the story of the sexton, Gabriel Grub,
'an ill-conditioned, cross-grained, surly fellow – a morose
and lonely man, who consorted with nobody but himself . . . and who eyed each merry face, as it passed
him by, with such a deep scowl of malice and ill-
humour, as it was difficult to meet, without feeling
something the worse for'. Grub's notion of how to pass
the evening of Christmas Eve most appropriately is to
labour in his profession by digging a grave. There he is
interrupted by goblins, who carry him off to a large
cavern, the palace of their king, where Grub is shown
some *tableaux vivants*. One group of pictures in particular showed a humble family of children welcoming
their father as he returns home, wet and weary, with
the snow clinging to his coat; and later the same
family are seen assembled in a small bedroom where the
youngest and fairest child lies dying. These pictures
and others are presented to show Grub that men who
work hard are happy, that women are often superior to
sorrow, adversity, and distress, and that men like himself, 'who snarled at the mirth and cheerfulness of
others, were the foulest weeds on the fair surface of the
earth'. The upshot is that when the goblins leave

[1] Chapter xxix.

him, Grub returns an altered and contented man.

Thus, in the December number of *Pickwick Papers*
and in Dickens's autumn meditations of 1843 are to be
found the principal ingredients of *A Christmas Carol*. It
is not difficult to recognize in Ebenezer Scrooge the
ill-conditioned, cross-grained Grub, who consorted
with nobody but himself; and the deep scowl of malice
and ill-humour, with which Grub eyed each merry
face, is elaborated in the surly reception Scrooge offers
to his jovial nephew. Just as Grub is carried off by
supernatural powers and shown representations of
what he is missing in life through his sulky behaviour,
so Scrooge is also transported. And the effect in each
case is the same: the surly man suffers a nursery-tale
transformation into a lover of his kind. Furthermore,
the picture which Grub sees of a humble family welcoming the return of their father on a winter evening
and, later, gathering round the deathbed of the
youngest child is a first sketch of the Cratchit family,
in which Bob Cratchit and Tiny Tim are already
faintly delineated. But whereas we are shown little
evidence of Grub's surliness and none of his reformed
character, we are permitted to see Scrooge in action
before and after his transformation; and whereas the
visions presented to Grub have no relation to the life
he has lived, the visions Scrooge sees are episodes in his
own life and in the lives of people he knows.

It is in the elaboration of the *Pickwick* story that
Dickens draws upon his recent meditations. Scrooge
is not only cross-grained; he is, as his name suggests, a
'screw', a 'squeezing, wrenching, grasping, scraping,
clutching, covetous old sinner'. Although there is no
humbug in him—indeed he constantly suspects it in
others—he belongs in fact with the self-seeking,
rapacious characters of *Martin Chuzzlewit*. Perhaps he is
most closely related to old Martin, who like Scrooge
also suffers a transformation. And at least two other
characters in the Christmas book bear some relation

to the characters in the novel: the washerwoman who steals the bedclothes from Scrooge's deathbed shares Mrs Gamp's rapacity, if not her more amiable qualities, and the loyalty of Bob Cratchit to the employer who oppresses him recalls Tom Pinch's loyalty to Mr Pecksniff.

We have seen how deeply Dickens had been shocked at the state of ignorance and neglect in the Ragged School at Saffron Hill, and how he claimed in his speech at the Manchester Athenaeum that ignorance is the most prolific parent of misery and crime. This theme also is echoed in the *Carol* when the Ghost of Christmas Present reveals a boy and a girl, 'yellow, meagre, ragged, scowling, wolfish; but prostrate, too, in their humility'. The boy, we are told, is Ignorance, the girl Want. 'Beware them both', says the Spirit, in the blank verse in which much of these books is unwittingly written; 'beware them both, and all of their degree; but most of all beware this boy, for on his brow I see that written which is Doom, unless the writing be erased. Deny it! . . . Slander those who tell it ye! Admit it for your factious purposes, and make it worse! And abide the end!' That is all we see of this cartoon figure in the *Carol*, but he will reappear more impressively in *The Haunted Man*, and more impressively still as Jo, the crossing-sweeper, in *Bleak House*.

It will be recalled that the Manchester merchant had no need to fear the banishment of ignorance, for the man who has improved his leisure will understand that 'the relations between himself and his employers involve a mutual duty and responsibility, [and] he will discharge his part of the implied contract cheerfully, faithfully, and honourably'. This is one of Dickens's favourite themes. It had been implicit in the relations of Mr Pickwick and Sam Weller, and explicit in the relations of the Cherryble brothers to Tim Linkinwater and Nicholas Nickleby. It is now to become prominent in the first three Christmas books, and in particular it supplies in the *Carol* that connexion between the surly man and his visions which had been lacking when Dickens treated the theme of transformation in the story of Gabriel Grub. Grub in his visions sees nothing connected with his own life, past or present; but Scrooge, the stingy employer, is first reminded how he was treated as an apprentice by his employer Fezziwig, is then shown what his treatment of Cratchit means to Cratchit's family, and lastly is made to recognize in the death of Tiny Tim, what the end of it is likely to be.

I believe this to be important in Dickens's development as a storyteller, since it is the first time he had attempted to direct his fertile imagination within the limits of a carefully constructed and premeditated plot. There is indeed no external evidence, in the shape of letters or draft sketch, to show what were his initial intentions. But the book as it stands bears the marks of constructive care at the outset. The opening picture of the unregenerate Scrooge, surly towards his clerk and his nephew, is balanced by the closing picture of Scrooge transformed, his transformation evident in his treatment of clerk and nephew; and the process of transformation is nicely graded in the visitations of the three spirits. This is the first occasion of Dickens discovering a plot sufficient to carry his message, and a plot conterminous with his message, a plot, that is to say, the whole of which bears upon his message and does not overlap it. A reviewer in *The Athenaeum* had happily remarked of *Martin Chuzzlewit* that 'events and vicissitudes *reel* rather than march to a conclusion'.[1] But in the *Carol*, though the reader may be called upon to rock with merriment or to weep, the trend of events is soberly and precisely measured. He had at last begun to keep a steadier eye upon the purpose and design of his work which was to characterize his novels from *Dombey and Son* onwards.

The connexion of Scrooge and the Cratchits is also important for the effect it had upon contemporary

[1] 20 July 1844, 665.

readers. Most of the reviewers accepted it in the spirit
of its writing. Thackeray, reviewing the book in *Fraser's*
Magazine, called it 'a National Benefit', and added:

> A Scotch philosopher, who nationally does not keep
> Christmas-day, on reading the book, sent out for
> a turkey, and asked two friends to dine–this is a
> fact! . . . Had the book appeared a fortnight
> earlier, all the prize cattle would have been gobbled
> up in pure love and friendship, Epping denuded of
> sausages, and not a turkey left in Norfolk.[1]

But it was not to be expected that the *Westminster*
Review, the organ of the philosophical radicals, would
treat economics so irresponsibly. While admitting that
Dickens had 'a strong perception . . . of the beauty
of generosity . . . the love of kind, the unselfish
attachment of man to man, and of man to men, and
also of men to man', the reviewer pointed out that 'the
great elementary truths on which man's physical well-
being, and consequently his mental well-being, must
depend', had apparently not been mastered. 'The
processes whereby poor men are to be enabled to earn
good wages, wherewith to buy turkeys for themselves,
does not enter into the account; indeed, it would quite
spoil the *dénouement* and all the generosity. Who went
without turkey and punch in order that Bob Cratchit
might get them–for, unless there were turkey and
punch in surplus, someone must go without–is a
disagreeable reflection kept wholly out of sight'.[2]

I do not want to overemphasize the importance of
this review, but we do know that Dickens read it and
embodied his retort in his next Christmas book, *The*
Chimes, in that passage where Mr Filer surprises Toby
Veck at his humble dinner and accuses him of snatching
his tripe out of the mouths of widows and orphans. This
is no more than a short episode in a book which restates

[1] xxix (1844) 169.
[2] From a review of R. H. Horne *A New Spirit of the Age* (1844)
xli, 374–6.

what Dickens liked to call his 'Carol philosophy', the nursery-tale philosophy that Evil is no match for Good, or Mightiness and Cunning for Bravery and Simplicity.

Nor is it the only episode in which the original can be somewhat dimly descried. I take it that Will Fern the farm labourer is driven to rick-burning because in this year, 1844, there had been serious outbreaks of incendiarism in the Eastern Counties; and I take it that Toby's daughter, Margaret, is driven (in Toby's vision) to drown her child, because Dickens had read that shocking Police Court case in the *Times* of 17 April 1844, where a woman had been sentenced to death for drowning her child. The woman had left the work-house because the child was maltreated, and she had taken work as a shirt-maker. But since she received no more than 1¾d. a shirt and could make no more than three a day, she left the job and went to invest all her small savings in buying ribands to make up caps; but on reaching the shop, she found that her purse had been stolen, and in desperation she attempted to drown herself and her child. The case is alluded to by Dickens in an ironical letter he wrote for *Hood's Magazine* in the character of a gentleman of the old school:

> There is only one judge who knows how to do his duty, now. He tried that revolutionary female the other day, who, though she was in full work (making shirts at three-halfpence a piece), had no pride in her country, but treasonably took it in her head, in the distraction of having been robbed of her easy earnings, to attempt to drown herself and her young child; and the glorious man went out of his way, sir, – out of his way – to call her up for instant sentence of Death; and to tell her she had no hope of mercy in this world.[1]

[1] 'Threatening letter to Thomas Hood,' May 1844. See 'Reprinted Pieces, etc'. National Edition of the Works of Charles Dickens, XXXIV, 374–5; or *Miscellaneous Papers by Dickens*, ed. B. W. Matz, I, 10 (Gadshill Edition, vol. XXXV).

I feel pretty sure that this is the origin of that episode in *The Chimes*; but there are other questions I should like to ask, before I could feel satisfied that I know enough about what Dickens was thinking at that time.[1]

But though its origins are not altogether clear, we are compensated by an outline sketch of *The Chimes* which Dickens sent to Forster on completing the first part of the book. In some respects the sketch is to be preferred to the completed work: the offence which Toby Veck has committed in doubting the right of the poor to their inheritance, in failing to recognize the native goodness in them, this is more clearly demonstrated in the sketch than in the book; and the concluding scene of his vision, in which a great sea rises, the sea of Time, and bears 'the alderman and such mud-worms of the earth away to nothing, dashing them to fragments in its fury', while 'Toby will climb a rock and hear the bells (now faded from his sight) pealing out upon the waters'–this sketch appears to offer opportunities to which in the event Dickens was not to rise. Forster's purpose in printing the sketch in his *Life of Dickens*[2] was to show how Dickens's fancy, when once on the wing, exerted its mastery over his first design. But what he failed to remark, acute critic though he was, is that once more Dickens had planned the whole work from beginning to end, that the plot is conterminous with the theme, and that the alterations are not of fundamental importance. I say that the alterations are not of fundamental importance even though one of them involves the introduction of Will Fern, an agricultural labourer and therefore a type of working man which Dickens rarely drew. But though a good deal of interest centres on Fern, he and his daughter (who is driven to prostitution) are no more

---

[1] Some of these questions are answered and more material on the background supplied, by Michael Slater in 'Dickens (and Forster) at Work on *The Chimes*', *Dickens Studies* II (1966) 106–40.
     [2] *Life*, IV, v.

than forceful illustrations of the theme which Dickens had already planned. They and the other alterations are in the nature of adjustments to the plan, rather than such wanton improvisations as his early novels had accustomed us to.

¶ The next two books, *The Cricket on the Hearth* and *The Battle of Life*, though they both contain some good and characteristic work, are below the other books in merit. Dickens appears to have had *The Cricket* in mind rather longer than the other books, for though he did not begin it until mid-October 1845 he had told Forster early in July of that year that he thought it would be 'a delicate and beautiful fancy for a Christmas book, making the Cricket a little household god–silent in the wrong and sorrow of the tale, and loud again when all went well and happy'.[1] Was that all? Had Dickens no more than that in his original conception of the tale? It would seem that he had not; and if we are right in thinking so, it would look as if there was not quite enough to make a book of the same size as the *Carol* and *The Chimes*. The book opens, as *The Chimes* had done, with a sort of Shandyan impromptu describing a contest between a kettle and a cricket to provide a fireside song of comfort.[2] The song provides a welcome for the village carrier, a middle-aged man, home from his rounds on a winter evening. Dickens then proceeds to paint the scene of comfort, love, and trustfulness in which the carrier lives with his young wife and baby. But he has brought back with him a stranger, an old man apparently, muffled up certainly, and probably in disguise. The stranger introduces a note of discord between the carrier and his wife, to which the cricket

[1] ibid., v, i.
[2] Incidentally, this overture was mercilessly parodied by W. E. Aytoun in *Blackwood's Magazine* (LX, November 1846, 601) in a passage which suggested to Lewis Carroll the opening paragraphs of *Through the Looking Glass*. See K. Tillotson 'Lewis Carroll and the Kitten on the Hearth' *English* VIII (1950) 136–8.

is sensitive; and the carrier becomes so jealous, when he sees the stranger kissing his wife, that he is moved to kill him. But he relents when he reflects on the disparity of age between himself and his wife, and is about to leave the field clear for his wife and her lover, when the explanation takes place: the stranger turns out to be the long-lost lover of a lady, a friend of the carrier's wife, who was about to be married to a neighbouring ogre. And so domestic trustfulness triumphs, and happiness is restored.

A trivial, commonplace story, you will say, barely sufficient to point the moral. I must agree; and I would point out that it is not even large enough to fill a Christmas book. The empty spaces, so to speak, have to be filled by episodes, some of them charming in themselves, but with no bearing, so far as I can see, upon the central theme. Of these the most prominent once more treats the relations of employer and employed. The ogre, who might have married the carrier's wife's friend, is a manufacturer of toys who maltreats his workman and his blind daughter. But except that our sympathies are invited for the down-trodden, nothing is made of the issue. Need I add that in the end the ogre suffers a transformation and distributes toys and Christmas cake with a lavish hand?

There is not enough evidence to speak with complete confidence. But what evidence we have points to a relapse into Dickens's old habits of setting out upon a story with but little view of the main track of his design. This, however, does not account for the weakness of the next book, *The Battle of Life*, a story of domestic unselfishness, in which the younger of two sisters leaves her home because she is brought to recognize that her elder sister conceals a love for the man whom the younger sister is engaged to marry. The trouble here, as Dickens subsequently admitted, was that he had chosen too short a form in which to elaborate a theme requiring lengthy treatment. He had laid down his plans with some care, but he had not left himself space to carry them out. 'I have written the first part', he told a correspondent at the end of September 1846; 'I know the end and upshot of the second; and the whole of the third (there are only three in all). I know the purport of each character, and the plain idea that each is to work out; and I have the principal effects sketched on paper'.[1] For none of his early novels could he have claimed so much as that.

But though *The Battle of Life* was an indisputable failure, it was not all lost labour. I think we can detect a few things salvaged from the wreck and put by for future use in the next novel *David Copperfield*. In the lawyer who makes a point of speaking for his partner, we see perhaps a hint of the relationship of Spenlow and Jorkins; in Clemency, the rough but devoted maid-servant, a first sketch of Peggotty; in the courage and self-sacrifice of the elder sister, some of the ingredients of Agnes Wickfield's character; and the difficulties in recognizing the promptings of the heart is a theme to which Dickens in *David Copperfield* was to give extended treatment.

¶ The last of the Christmas books was *The Haunted Man*. It was begun about six months after the close of *Dombey and Son*, and picks up the theme of that novel's concluding chapters. Mr Dombey's pride has had its fall, Florence returns to rescue him—another trans-formed man—from the house of many memories, and all ends in forgiveness and reconciliation. When we first meet the learned chemist Redlaw, he is a haunted man brooding upon a past from which he cannot escape. There are differences, of course, between Redlaw and Dombey, differences appropriate to the position in the story: Redlaw at the outset of his adventures, Dombey at the close of his. And there are differences appropriate to the scope of the book, one being a twenty-monthly

[1] *Letters*, I, 791.

serial and the other a short Christmas 'fancy'. Redlaw
therefore scans the past with a bitterness which *future*
events are to correct, while Dombey scans it with a
remorse which *past* events have brought; and while the
scope of a long novel permits an extensive report of
Dombey's brooding, the briefness of a Christmas book
demands a short cut; and the supernatural tradition in
which Dickens had been working suggests for that
short cut a dialogue between the haunted man and a
ghost, who represents 'the darker presentment of
himself embodied in [his] bitter recollections'. These
differences of presentation conceal the essential similarity between Redlaw and Mr Dombey, in that each
must be released from his unhappy bondage of past
memories by accepting the bad with the good, and
that each is released by the intervention of a 'good
angel', one of the 'simply meek' who in Dickens have
always something to teach the 'worldly wise'.

The full title of the book is *The Haunted Man and the
Ghost's Bargain*. That bargain is that the ghost will
cease to haunt Redlaw, that Redlaw will cease to
remember his sorrows and wrongs, provided that he
carries this imperviousness to the past in a sort of
Midas-touch to other people. Readers of *Dombey and
Son* would remember that that was not the way Mr
Dombey had learned to conquer his bitter recollections,
and the Christmas book itself hints in its opening pages
that the memory has an important function. As so
often happens in Dickens's tales, the simple have a
wisdom denied to the sophisticated. So, here, too, there
is a simple superannuated porter in the college where
Redlaw lives, whose memory in his old age is his great
stand-by. The old man's life has not been altogether
happy: most of his children have died, his wife has
gone too, 'and my son, George (our eldest, who was
her pride more than all the rest!) is fallen very low:
but I can see them, when I look here, alive and healthy,
as they used to be in those days; and I can see him,

thank God, in his innocence. It's a blessed thing to me, at eighty-seven'. Accordingly the old man has adopted for his motto the words on a scroll beneath a portrait in the great hall of the college, 'Lord! keep my memory green!'

But this simple wisdom is lost upon the learned Redlaw, who sallies out, altruistically, to help mankind with his Midas-touch of forgetfulness. As we watch his progress, we see that a wave of destruction follows in his wake. Those he meets are all suffering in some respect, either in body, or in estate. But each has managed to win a calm of mind in his sufferings by the recollection of some act of human sympathy. At Redlaw's touch all changes, and each when deprived of his memories becomes a querulous egotist, living merely for himself and for the moment. Only two persons are preserved from the bane of Redlaw's touch, Milly, the old porter's daughter-in-law, and a savage child who has been an outcast from kindness since his birth. The child, in whom the sense of grief as a moral emotion has never been awakened, is the only companion Redlaw has left on earth. That is the situation at the end of the second part. But at the beginning of the third, Milly, is used to set up a contrary motion. As she passes through the groups which Redlaw has affected, the strength of her simple affections restores them by bringing back their power of memory both for good and for ill. Even Redlaw himself discovers from Milly that the ability to weep with those that weep is the only condition on which he can partake in their joys. And the moral is the moral that pervades the last chapters of *Dombey and Son*. We can take it in Dickens's own words: 'Of course my point', he writes to Forster, 'is that bad and good are inextricably linked in remembrance, and that you could not choose the enjoyment of recollecting only the good. To have all the best of it you must remember the worst also'.[1]

[1] *Life*, VI, iv.

My summary will have indicated how this book partakes of the Christmas spirit and the Christmas philosophy of the others in the series. But that is incidental to my purpose, which is once more to show Dickens's constructive powers at work. The pattern in this little book is a good deal more complex than in the others, and must (I think) have been worked out ahead of composition. The antithesis between Milly and Redlaw upon which the plot turns is presented in the first episode and is carefully developed in those two contrary motions, the wave of destruction which follows Redlaw, and the wave of healing which accompanies Milly. Furthermore, the fatality of the ghost's bargain is apparent to those who have listened to the simple old man repeating the words from the scroll on the picture, 'Lord! keep my memory green!' This is one of those gnomic sayings upon which Dickens is now beginning to rely for keeping his readers reminded of what is at issue while he teases them with the complexities of plot. There is a notable instance of this practice in the oft-repeated words in *Dombey and Son*, 'Let him remember it in that room, years to come'; but I do not recollect any earlier instances of the device–which is one more illustration of the care which Dickens is now applying to matters of constructional technique.

The Haunted Man also permits us to observe how much more skilful Dickens has become in the use of the supernatural. We are prepared for supernatural figures in a Christmas tale, and no one will therefore be inclined to question the appropriateness of the goblins who carry off Gabriel Grub in the *Pickwick* story. But they have no significance, they are meaningless agents of Grub's transformation. It is therefore a welcome advance to find that the supernatural figures in *A Christmas Carol* are moral agents with an ulterior, though very obvious, significance. They resemble the allegorical figures in a newspaper cartoon, who bear their names clearly printed on their garments; just as the two children whom the Ghost of Christmas Present shows to Scrooge are also clearly labelled 'Ignorance' and 'Want'. But the Ghost in *The Haunted Man* is nothing so obvious. He is Mr Hyde to Redlaw's Dr Jekyll, and provides Dickens with an essential and appropriate short cut in representing an internal dialogue, just as Redlaw's supernatural powers, his baneful, Midas-touch, provides an essential short cut—essential in so short a book—for representing his influence upon others.

And the boy labelled 'Ignorance' in *A Christmas Carol*, what has he become? He has become in *The Haunted Man* a clearly recognizable savage slum child. There are no labels to be seen on his ragged clothes, but when placed side by side with Redlaw we recognize that he represents a creature in whom no emotions have been aroused except those derived from pain and hunger.

This is a step in advance of anything which Dickens had hitherto contrived; but if we care to look still further ahead, to *Bleak House*, we shall see him extending these experiments. The supernatural still has its use, though it is limited to the step on the Ghost's Walk at Chesney Wold which warns the Dedlocks of the coming of calamity or disgrace, and serves to prepare the reader for the catastrophe ahead. And the slum child now becomes a fully realized character, Jo the crossing sweeper; but he is used, just as the other boys were used, to symbolize the dangers to society of leaving savagery, dirt, and ignorance untouched in the slums. Esther Summerson catching the smallpox indirectly from Jo is an episode which carries much the same lesson as Dickens is trying to teach through the two boys of the Christmas books, but the lesson is more forcible because it has been more perfectly symbolized. Yet one may doubt whether Dickens could have perfected that highly important element in his art, his symbolism, without first making these Christmas experiments.

The Haunted Man was the last of the Christmas books. I do not know why nothing was written for Christmas 1849; but when Christmas 1850 arrived, Dickens had established his periodical *Household Words* and contributed to it a Christmas number called 'A Christmas Tree'; and every year thereafter until 1867 he made a similar contribution. These 'Christmas Stories', as they are called, constitute a distinct group with problems of form which must be examined in their periodical setting. I shall be satisfied if I have managed to convince the reader that the earlier group have an interest apart from any intrinsic value they may possess, in that they show us a great novelist at work perfecting his narrative art for the triumphs to come.

1951

The Serial Publication of Dickens's Novels
Martin Chuzzlewit *and* Little Dorrit

Nowadays we are accustomed to novels being published in single volumes, but 120 years ago this form of publication was unusual. In the eighteenth century novels had appeared in five, or even in nine volumes, and by the time of Scott and Jane Austen the favourite number was three or four. The prices varied; but it was not uncommon to charge as much as half-a-guinea a volume, which made novel-reading exceedingly expensive for those who did not belong to a circulating library. These were the conditions ruling when Dickens began to write. His first novel, *Pickwick Papers*, shows him attempting to reach a larger number of readers by cutting the price to suit their pockets, and the method he chose was to publish in serial.

During the course of his career he tried several types of serial. Thus *Oliver Twist* was published monthly in *Bentley's Miscellany*; *The Old Curiosity Shop* and *Barnaby Rudge* were published weekly in *Master Humphrey's Clock*; *Hard Times* and *Great Expectations* appeared weekly, the first in *Household Words* and the second in *All The Year Round*; while for *A Tale of Two Cities* he adopted a simultaneous publication of weekly and monthly issues. For the remainder of his novels he chose the monthly serial part, which he had first used in *Pickwick*. It is with this form only that I shall concern myself.

The serial form of the monthly part was determined during the writing of *Pickwick*. Dickens himself tells us of the decision to increase the number of pages after the first two issues from twenty-four a month (or three half-sheets) to thirty-two (or two whole-sheets); and thirty-two pages was always thereafter to be his monthly stint. This provided enough room for three or four chapters; never more, except in the final 'double' number, though in *Pickwick*, nos. X and XII, and *Chuzzlewit*, nos. II, IV, V, and VII there are only two. There are no monthly numbers consisting of a single chapter; and the six I have named are the only numbers with two. The appeal of three or four chapters seems originally to have been that they gave the opportunity for the diversity of material which Dickens was accustomed to supplying in the magazine. Thus the third number of *Pickwick* (chapters vi-viii), which was the first of thirty-two pages, is designedly miscellaneous in content, with Mr Tupman's amorous adventure, the sporting humour of Mr Winkle's shooting and the cricket match, some comic oratory, a set of verses ('The Ivy Green'), and a grim short story of 'The Convict's Return'. Few numbers in the later novels so obviously imitate a magazine's contents, though in *Chuzzlewit* he will still offer his readers a magazine sketch from time to time. 'Town and Todgers's' (chapter ix) in no. IV clearly recalls the original Boz, and that manner is seen only a little less clearly in the proceedings of the Anglo-Bengalee Disinterested Loan and Life Assurance Company of no. XI (chapters xxvii-xxix). Sketches of this kind disappear from the novels after *Chuzzlewit*, a sign that Dickens by that time was making a clearer distinction between the novel and the magazine.

But though these sketches disappear in the interests of a more closely integrated novel, Dickens still usually likes to see his three or four chapters as an opportunity for variety of incident and manner. He will occasionally give us homogeneous numbers; and the three American numbers, VII, IX, and XIII (chapters xvi-xvii, xxi-xxiii, xxxiii-xxxv), are notable instances, for these instalments are solely concerned with the experiences of Martin and Mark Tapley in the United States; but in contrast with these there is the variety offered by such a number as VIII (chapters xviii-xx), which contains the death of Anthony Chuzzlewit, the first introduction of Mrs Gamp, and Jonas's engagement to Mercy Pecksniff. Scarcely less diverse is no. XVIII (chapters xlviii-l), which begins with Young Martin's early morning visit to Tom Pinch and the revelations of Lewsome, goes on to Mrs Gamp's quarrel with Mrs Prig, and ends with Old Martin announcing himself to Tom Pinch as his employer.

In *Little Dorrit* the only number to match the American numbers of *Chuzzlewit* in homogeneity is no. XVIII (Book II, chapters xxvii-xxix), which is devoted to Arthur Clennam's experiences in the Marshalsea. Diversity, then, would seem to be Dickens's policy, as he faced the writing of the great majority of his monthly instalments; and though he may have begun by aiming at variety in imitation of the magazine, he was induced to continue to keep this end in view by the varied strands of his plots.

Though nowadays we normally read Dickens's novels without paying attention to their serial divisions, it is important for us to recognize that that was impossible for his first readers. They were originally confined to their thirty-two pages, which they could easily read on the evening of publication. Their reading was therefore subject to long and frequent interruptions; and though they must certainly have had the impression of watching the development of a single work of art, to which each instalment made its contribution, they must also have been aware that each number had its identity—its physical identity, obviously, when bound by its green paper covers, but its

identity as a structural unit as well. This would have
been at its clearest on the rare occasions when the
contents were homogeneous; but elsewhere there would
have been the impression of a slow, gradual unfolding
of the plot. And Dickens helps his readers to accept
the identity of the unit by paying attention to the
manner in which it begins and ends. He seems to have
felt that the ending was the more important, for he
never panders to readers' forgetfulness by summariz-
ing past events, he rarely even refers to them, and he
never uses such a phrase as 'last month' or 'in the last
number'. I quote a few instances from *Chuzzlewit* to
show the utmost he is prepared to do in helping his
reader pick up the thread after a month's interval:

> No. IX. The knocking at Mr Pecksniff's door,
> though loud enough, bore no resemblance what-
> ever to the noise of an American railway train at
> full speed. It may be well to begin the present
> chapter with this frank admission, lest the reader
> should imagine that the sounds now deafening
> this history's ears have any connection . . .[1]
> No. XII. As the surgeon's first care after
> amputating a limb is to take up the arteries the
> cruel knife has severed, so it is the duty of this
> history, which in its remorseless course has cut
> from the Pecksniffian trunk its right arm, Mercy,
> to look to the parent stem, and see how in all its
> various ramifications it got on without her.[2]
> No. XVII. Tom Pinch and his sister having to
> part, for the dispatch of the morning's business,
> immediately after the dispersion of the other actors
> in the scene upon the wharf with which the reader
> has already been acquainted, had no opportunity
> of discussing the subject at that time. But Tom,
> in his solitary office, etc. etc.[3]

But the *conclusion* of each number is a different matter.

---

[1] Chapter xxi.   [2] Chapter xxx.   [3] Chapter xlv.

In the first number of *Pickwick*, Dickens had been constrained to bring the number to a close in the middle of a chapter; but elsewhere he always contrived that the end of a number and the end of a chapter should coincide. But the end of the final chapter of a number necessarily involves a longer pause than the end of any other chapter provides, and how is that to be treated? It is popularly believed that the serial writer tries to reach a moment of apprehension, that he suspends his narrative at an emotional climax, leaving his readers in anxiety for what is to come. There are some instances of these melodramatic endings in *Chuzzlewit*, notably VIII, where Tom Pinch announces the arrival of old Martin in Mr Pecksniff's village, while Jonas is in his house:

'Dear, dear!' cried Tom, 'what have I done? I hoped it would be a pleasant surprise, sir. I thought you would like to know.'

But at that moment a loud knocking was heard at the hall-door.[1]

And X, where Chuffey greets the newly-married Mercy:

'You are not married?' he said, eagerly. 'Not married?'

'Yes. A month ago. Good Heaven, what is the matter?'

He answered nothing was the matter; and turned from her. But in her fear and wonder, turning also, she saw him raise his trembling hands above his head, and heard him say:

'Oh! woe, woe, woe, upon this wicked house!'

It was her welcome,–HOME.[2]

More grossly melodramatic is the conclusion of XVII with Jonas's return to London after the murder of Montague Tigg:

Whether he attended to their talk, or tried to think of other things, or talked himself, or held his peace, or resolutely counted the dull tickings of a hoarse

[1] Chapter xx.   [2] Chapter xxvi.

clock at his back, he always lapsed, as if a spell
were on him, into eager listening. For he knew
it must come; and his present punishment, and
torture, and distraction, were, to listen for its
coming.
Hush![1]

There is nothing equivalent to that in *Little Dorrit*. The
closest in excitement is the end of IX, where at last
Pancks reveals to Clennam the result of his researches:

We've been at it, night and day, for I don't
know how long. Mr Rugg, you know how long?
Never mind. Don't say. You'll only confuse me.
You shall tell her, Mr Clennam. Not till we give
you leave. Where's that rough total, Mr Rugg?
Oh! Here we are! There, sir! That's what you'll
have to break to her. That man's your Father of
the Marshalsea![2]

But whereas the three *Chuzzlewit* numbers were termi-
nated in a mood of apprehension, the *Dorrit* number
ends on a climax of excitement. It would take too
long to classify all the terminations, and would not
serve much purpose. There are those which, while
clearly pointing to future action, arrive at an acceptable
moment of rest; such is Mark Tapley's view of the
Land of Liberty at the conclusion of the bad Atlantic
crossing in no. VIII. There is the picturesque ending
of *Dorrit*, no. III, where we see in the light of dawn
John Baptist Cavalletto running away from his patron
(Book I, chapter xi), or the more contrived grouping of
Little Dorrit and Maggy sleeping in St George's vestry
at the end of no. IV (chapter xiv), and John Chivery's
new inscription for his gravestone at the end of V
(chapter xviii). My point is that the end is recognized
and designed in various ways as a suitable point of rest,
even though the rest is sometimes charged with apprehension.

Yet though each number had its separate identity,

[1] Chapter xlvii.   [2] Book I, chapter xxxi.

it was planned to make a contribution to a larger whole. In the 1837 Preface to *Pickwick*, Dickens describes what he was attempting to do:

The publication of the book in monthly numbers, containing only thirty-two pages in each, rendered it an object of paramount importance that, while the different incidents were linked together by a chain of interest strong enough to prevent their appearing unconnected or impossible, the general design should be so simple as to sustain no injury from this detached and desultory form of publication, extending over no fewer than twenty months. In short, it was necessary – or it appeared so to the Author – that every number should be, to a certain extent, complete in itself, and yet that the whole twenty numbers, when collected, should form one tolerably harmonious whole, each leading to the other by a gentle and not unnatural progress of adventure.

It is obvious that in a work published with a view to such considerations, no artfully interwoven or ingeniously complicated plot can with reason be expected.

So far as organization was concerned, he was not setting himself a very exacting task in *Pickwick*. One number more or less than twenty for that novel would not have mattered very much. But still, twenty numbers had been stipulated, perhaps for no better reason than that twenty shillings make one pound, and he was determined not to alter the decision. The original advertisement had specified 'about twenty numbers', and an Address prefaced to *Pickwick* no. x declared his 'intention to adhere to his original pledge'.

The length of *Pickwick* determined the length of every subsequent monthly novel, except *Edwin Drood*, designed for completion in twelve, and this exact prescription became an important factor as soon as he began to pay more attention to plot. This happened in the very next novel, *Nicholas Nickleby*. Although the preface still shows him thinking in terms of the periodical essay and using the words of an eighteenth-century periodical essayist to justify his work, it was during the progress of that novel that he began to meditate a plot. It is certainly neither 'artful' nor 'ingenious', and it in no way corresponds to the theme of the book; but there it is, manifest for the first time in no. XIV (chapters xliii–xlv), when Dickens has only six months more in front of him, and must devise some means of bringing the book to a close.

In *Martin Chuzzlewit* and in each of the later novels, Dickens set out with a theme in mind and devised a plot to help him in expounding that theme. His success in *Chuzzlewit* is not so striking as in the later novels, but there is no doubting his intentions: 'I set out, on this journey which is now concluded, with the design of exhibiting, in various aspects, the commonest of all vices'; so he writes in the original preface, and the last words of the first Number explain what that commonest of all vices is: ' "Oh self, self, self! Every man for himself, and no creature for me!" Universal self! Was there nothing of its shadow in these reflections, and in the history of Martin Chuzzlewit, on his own showing?'[1] And that Dickens has kept that theme before him, we have at least his word in the original preface, written after completing the novel:

> I have endeavoured in the progress of this Tale, to
> resist the temptation of the current Monthly
> Number, and to keep a steadier eye upon the general
> purpose and design. With this object in view, I
> have put a strong constraint upon myself from
> time to time, in many places; and I hope the story
> is the better for it, now.

The theme demanded more attention to design than he had paid in *Pickwick* and *Nickleby*. It was not merely a question of illustrating aspects of selfishness

[1] Chapter iii.

in such characters as Pecksniff, Jonas, and the two Martins, and of unselfishness in Mark Tapley, John Westlock, and Tom Pinch, but the action must also serve to punish Pecksniff and Jonas, and to work a cure upon the two Martins. The punishment of Pecksniff requires the deception played upon him by Old Martin, and preparations are made for that as early as chapter vi, the first chapter of no. III, where Pecksniff arranges to go up to London with his daughters at Old Martin's behest.

At what point Dickens decided upon the manner of Jonas's punishment, it is difficult to determine; but if he foresaw the murder of Montague Tigg as soon as Jonas became involved in the Anglo-Bengalee, we must place it no earlier than no. XI (chapters xxvii–xxix). But the murder of Tigg is no more than an exacerbation of Jonas's offences. The death of Anthony occurs in no. VIII, and the first indications of Jonas's distaste for his father appear in chapter xi, the first chapter of no. V, but not, I think, any earlier. It is also part of Jonas's function to ruin Pecksniff, his father-in-law, and this he does in no. XVI, in a scene which Thackeray especially admired, where Jonas triumphs at the very moment when Pecksniff thinks he is achieving his masterpiece of dissembling (chapter xliv). But for Jonas to be placed in the necessary relationship with Pecksniff, the marriage with Mercy must be arranged, and that takes us back to no. IV (chapters ix–x).

Now to speak of these incidents being designed implies some premeditation on Dickens's part; yet Forster tells us that Dickens began his work hurriedly, altered his course at the opening, and saw little at that moment of the main track of his design. The letters substantiate Forster in part at least. There was no prolonged period of incubation. Throughout the late summer and autumn of 1842, he was fully occupied with *American Notes*, which was not disposed of until the end of October. He then immediately went upon a

short trip to Cornwall to look for the opening scene of a
new book. Whatever his scheme was, it was found
impracticable. His correspondence with John Leech in
the first week of November shows him in the process of
considering it and turning it down. Yet as early as 12
November he writes to Miss Coutts that he is 'in the
agonies of plotting and contriving a new book', by 8
December the first Number was 'nearly done', and on
31 December it was published.[1] There was certainly
little enough time for premeditation. But, as I have
already said, the theme of self is propounded in the
first Number, and there Pecksniff opens his designs on
Old Martin. Old Martin's plans are laid in no. III
(chapters vi-viii), and Jonas plans to marry Mercy in
no. IV (chapters ix-x). There is room enough for growth
under his hands in the very process of writing, and I
feel doubtful whether, for example, he foresaw the
possibilities of Jonas deceiving Pecksniff in no. XVI
(chapters xlii-xliv) when he chose a wife for Jonas in
IV. But my point is this, that from an early stage in
the novel he has to take his decisions knowing he has
about 624 pages at his disposal, divided into twenty
monthly parts. Obviously Old Martin must reveal
himself to Pecksniff in his true colours in the last
Number. How much should be disposed of before then?
Young Martin should be cured, should seek to reconcile
himself with his grandfather, and should be rebuffed by
Pecksniff. Therefore Young Martin must be brought
back from America soon enough to allow for that. In
fact he returns in XIII (in chapter xxxv), though that
may have been less because he needed Martin in
England, than because he had grown tired of America.

The unfolding of the subplot relating to Jonas may
well have caused more trouble. Though the Anglo-
Bengalee complications are opened as early as no. XI
(in chapter xxvii), there is no room to develop them
until the end of XIV (chapters xxxvi-xxxviii), partly

[1] *Letters*, I, 487, 493, 497.

because Martin has to be brought back from America, but largely because Dickens has allowed Tom Pinch to become a pet character and to steal more than his share of space. But once the Anglo-Bengalee is resumed in XIV, there is obviously little time to spare. In XV (chapters xxxix-xli) Jonas is stopped from making off to the Continent, in XVI (chapters xlii-xliv) he goes down to Wiltshire to seduce Pecksniff, in XVII (chapters xlv-xlvii) he murders Montague Tigg, in XVIII (chapters xlviii-l) Lewsome reveals what he knows, and in the first chapter (li) of XIX/XX Jonas commits suicide. It looks as though Dickens has kept a sharp eye on the decreasing number of pages at his disposal from no. XIV onwards.

If he had lived in the previous generation, I suspect that he would have found his task a little easier, since the convention of the three-volume novel acted as a constant reminder to a novelist of the point which he had reached in his story. We can observe even so comparatively reckless a novelist as Scott taking his bearings as he moves from one volume to the next. But a novel of 624 large octavo pages is an unwieldy size; and even when divided into units of thirty-two it seems to require some larger grouping to make its form felt. After *Martin Chuzzlewit* Dickens was to write three more novels with no other division than chapter and number. These were *Dombey and Son*, *David Copperfield*, and *Bleak House*. But during the writing of his next novel, *Hard Times*, a weekly serial, he made a note in his memoranda, which reads 'Republish in three books? 1. Sowing. 2. Reaping. 3. Garnering.' The device of dividing into books was not a new one. Fielding had adopted it from the epic in *Joseph Andrews*, and many novelists had followed him. What perhaps attracted Dickens's attention was Thackeray's refinement in *Esmond* (1852) of not merely numbering his books, as the custom was, but of naming them too. At any rate when *Hard Times* was reissued in volume form, it was divided into three books with the titles I have mentioned; and except for *Edwin Drood*, every subsequent novel was divided into books, even in the serial issue.

The most attractive example is *Great Expectations*, which is divided into three equal parts of nineteen chapters, representing the three stages of Pip's expectations. The first stage ends with the announcement of his expectations and his move to London, and the second ends with the return of Pip's unknown benefactor, the convict Magwitch. Who can doubt that the reader's sense of the larger movements in the story is assisted by these divisions; and who can doubt, as he contemplates this threefold structure, that all was carefully planned from the beginning?

Little Dorrit[1] is also divided into books, 'Book the First. Poverty', 'Book the Second. Riches', but this was not part of the original conception of the novel. Professor Kathleen Tillotson[2] has shown that the original title of the novel, *Nobody's Fault*, was abandoned, in all probability, during the writing of chapter xii, the first chapter of no. IV, not long before the publication of no. I, and a new title, *Little Dorrit*, was substituted. The sub-title, 'Book the First. Poverty', was added in proof. It could not, of course, have had any relevance to the original title, *Nobody's Fault*; but once the change to *Little Dorrit* was made, probably in the middle of September 1855, Dickens could afford to reconsider his bearings in the light of the new title, and adopt a notion expressed to Forster in a letter of 16 September, when he was beginning to work upon no. III (chapters ix-xi):

> There is an enormous outlay in the Father of the
> Marshalsea chapter, in the way of getting a great

---

[1] A fuller account of the serial publication of this novel may be found in 'Dickens' Monthly Number Plans for *Little Dorrit*', Paul D. Herring *Modern Philology* 64, 22–63 (August 1966).

[2] *Dickens at Work* (1957) 231.

lot of matter into a small space. I am not quite
resolved, but I have a great idea of overwhelming
that family with wealth. Their condition would be
very curious. I can make Dorrit [he means Little
Dorrit] very strong in the story, I hope.[1]

In its timing the decision is comparable to that major
decision in *Chuzzlewit* to entangle Pecksniff in Old
Martin's toils, and one might argue what difference
the comparative lateness of the decision had upon the
earlier numbers already written. But irrespective of
that, I think it is clear that once the decision has been
made and 'Book the First. Poverty' inscribed in proof,
Old Dorrit will be released from the Marshalsea at the
end of no. X (in chapter xxxvi), and Dickens must take
up his dispositions accordingly. On this we have
additional evidence for *Little Dorrit* denied to us for
Martin Chuzzlewit, and that is the so-called 'Number-
Plans', the memoranda which Dickens wrote to assist
him in designing each Number. They show this
recognition of a turning-point in no. X. In the Number-
Plan for no. VII, chapter xxiii, we read 'Pancks. Pave
the way for his discovery, and the end of book [the]
1st'; in VIII, chapter xxix, 'Glimpse of Little Dorrit and
Pancks, to carry through'; and in IX (chapters xxx-
xxxii), the general direction reads 'Tip?-Fanny?-Father
and Uncle?-Carry through, except the Uncle-Family
Spirit—working up to what they are likely to be in a
higher station', and for chapter xxxii, where Clennam
visits Little Dorrit in the Marshalsea, the note reads,
'Prepare for the time to come, in that room, long afterwards. Pancks, immensely excited—strong preparation
for the end of the book'.

There are two advantages of the division into two
books, which these memoranda seem to me to indicate.
One is that dispositions can be taken with a nearer end
in view and with a more manageable quantity of
numbers in hand. Instead of that distant and crowded

[1] *Life*, VIII, i.

no. XIX-XX, there is the more immediate climax in
no. X to plan for. And on the other side of that dividing
line, planning can be carried on within more manageable limits. With Clennam and Little Dorrit to be
married in XIX-XX and the end of the old house and
Rigaud, Flintwinch, and Mrs Clennam, it seems
suitable to place Clennam in prison in the penultimate
number. Accordingly I am inclined to read as a fairly
early decision, taken well before the writing of XVIII,
the two general memoranda in that Number-Plan for
Contents:

> Clennam in the Marshalsea, and lodged in the old
> room. Little Dorrit comes to him in the old dress,
> and attended by Maggy in the old way. The
> Merdle Image smashed?

And I am fortified in the view that those plans, though
written in the Number-Plan for XVIII, were made well
in advance of no. XVIII, by a reply to the Merdle
question: 'Done last Number'. Yes, of course; most of
no. XVII (chapters xxiii-xxvi) had been given to
smashing 'The Merdle Image'. Dickens could not
possibly have forgotten it; and the only explanation of
this curious entry in the XVIIIth Number-Plan must
be that Dickens had at one time resolved that the
smash should occur there, not reflecting perhaps (or
not deciding) that since Arthur Clennam was to be
involved in the smash, the smash must occur before he
is shown in the Marshalsea, to which of course he was
sent as a bankrupt.

But whether we agree with these speculations or not
at least we may allow that this long-term miscalculation
about the death of Merdle, slight as it is, provides
evidence of foresight directed to the planning of the
novel, number by number. The Merdle entries in this
second book, in particular, show the deliberate march
of controlled events. They begin in XII (chapters v–vii)
with 'Pave the way – with the first stone – to Mr Merdle's ruining everybody? Yes.' In XIII (chapters viii-xi)

he is merely reviewed with the memorandum 'Mr Merdle? Next time.' And next time, that is, in XIV (chapters xii-xiv), he is triumphantly entered with a 'Yes', triply underlined, and the note 'Mr Merdle's Barnacle dinner, for the great patriotic purpose of making Young Sparkler a Lord of the Treasury.' The first memorandum for XV (chapters xv-xviii) reads 'Mr Dorrit to come to London, Invest his property with Mr Merdle, and return full of plans, never to be accomplished. Tone on to his dying in next Number.' XVI (chapters xix-xxii) merely notes 'Pave on to Mrs Merdle's great dinner', which is of course accomplished in XVII (chapters xxiii-xxvi), where the memorandum reads 'Merdles? Yes. His suicide and demolition.'

The second advantage in the division of the novel into two books, is that it permits some contrasted movements, some parallel scenes, and contrived ironies. The most obvious is the passage from poverty to riches in Book 1, and from riches to poverty in Book 2. We must surely also notice the assembly of travellers gathered at Marseilles in the opening scene of Book 1 matched by the assembly of travellers at the Great St Bernard in the opening scene of Book 2, and Clennam bringing comfort to Little Dorrit in the Marshalsea at the end of Book 1 matched by the reversal of roles at the end of Book 2 where it is Clennam that is in the Marshalsea and Little Dorrit that brings him comfort there. No less obvious is the irony of Mr Dorrit's being freed from imprisonment in the first Book, only to become the prisoner of polite society in the Second, with Mrs General as jailer.

Certainly the pointing of these contrasts and ironies is assisted by the two-book structure. But there are themes which appear to be unaffected by that structure and to be developed irrespective of it. The fall of the old house and the discovery of Mrs Clennam's secret are pursued over the full range of twenty numbers rather than within the limited scope of two books of ten numbers each. Some continuity must be expected; but perhaps we all wish that Dickens could have devised something a little more memorable for the connecting thread. At any rate there is some satisfaction that Dickens himself could not trust himself to recollect all the relevant details. The Number-Plans show that before he sat down to write the final double number, he had to set out the whole Clennam-Flintwinch-Dorrit entanglement in note form with page references back to his printed text. These he called his 'Memoranda for working the Story round', 'Retrospective' and 'Prospective'. Ironically his last enquiry reads 'What was the appeal to Mrs Clennam. Do Not Forget?'

1958

Index